2023 Easy Air Fryer

Cookbook for Beginners UK

2000+ Days Delicious, Quick & Budget-Friendly Recipes Book incl. Snacks, Side Dishes, Desserts, etc. - Using UK Measurements & Ingredients

Liedia Parkinson

Table of Contents

INTRODUCTION 1

To Know Your Air Fryer 2
Why Air Frying? 3
Tips for Using 4
Maintaining the Air Fryer 5

Chapter 1 Breakfasts 6

Denver Omelette 7
Keto Quiche 7
Bourbon Vanilla French Toast 7
Sausage and Egg Breakfast Burrito 8
Cheddar Soufflés 8
Pancake Cake 8
Gyro Breakfast Patties with Tzatziki 8
Simple Cinnamon Toasts 9
Veggie Frittata 9
Pancake for Two 9
Nutty Granola 9
Mushroom-and-Tomato Stuffed Hash Browns 9
Sausage Stuffed Peppers 10
Fried Chicken Wings with Waffles 10
Poached Eggs on Whole Grain Avocado Toast 10
Canadian Bacon Muffin Sandwiches 10
Butternut Squash and Ricotta Frittata 11
Honey-Apricot Granola with Greek Yoghurt 11
Smoky Sausage Patties 11
All-in-One Toast 11
Spinach and Bacon Roll-ups 12
Parmesan Sausage Egg Muffins 12
Bacon, Cheese, and Avocado Melt 12
Meritage Eggs 12
Baked Peach Oatmeal 12

Chapter 2 Poultry 13

Chicken Schnitzel Dogs 14
Greek Chicken Souvlaki 14
Crunchy Chicken with Roasted Carrots 14
Chipotle Aioli Wings 15
Teriyaki Chicken Legs 15
Chicken Nuggets 15
Chicken Wellington 15
Golden Tenders 16
Apricot-Glazed Turkey Tenderloin 16
Sweet and Spicy Turkey Meatballs 16
Fiesta Chicken Plate 16
Cheese-Encrusted Chicken Tenderloins with Peanuts 17
Italian Flavour Chicken Breasts with Roma Tomatoes 17
Korean Honey Wings 17
Chicken Legs with Leeks 17
Indian Fennel Chicken 18
Porchetta-Style Chicken Breasts 18
Chicken Patties 18
Tex-Mex Chicken Breasts 18
Chicken with Pineapple and Peach 19
Brazilian Tempero Baiano Chicken Drumsticks 19
Chicken and Vegetable Fajitas 19
Lemon Chicken with Garlic 19
Chicken, Courgette, and Spinach Salad 20
Buttermilk-Fried Drumsticks 20

Chapter 3 Beef, Pork, and Lamb 21

Crescent Dogs 22
Beef Mince Taco Rolls..22
Sesame Beef Lettuce Tacos 22
BBQ Pork Steaks...23
Onion Pork Kebabs 23
Almond and Caraway Crust Steak 23
Steak with Bell Pepper 23
Italian Lamb Chops with Avocado Mayo.............23
Mozzarella Stuffed Beef and Pork Meatballs.......24
Italian Sausages with Peppers and Onions...........24
Fillet with Crispy Shallots...................................24
Chuck Kebab with Rocket 24
Blackened Steak Nuggets...................................25

Herb-Roasted Beef Tips with Onions 25
Parmesan-Crusted Pork Chops...........................25
Beef and Goat Cheese Stuffed Peppers 25
Lemony Pork Loin Chop Schnitzel......................25
Bacon-Wrapped Pork Tenderloin 26
Steaks with Walnut-Blue Cheese Butter 26
Cajun Bacon Pork Loin Fillet 26
Panko Crusted Calf's Liver Strips........................26
Sausage-Stuffed Peppers 27
Goat Cheese-Stuffed Bavette Steak 27
Greek Lamb Rack 27
Cheese Pork Chops...27

Chapter 4 Fish and Seafood 28

Crab-Stuffed Avocado Boats 29
Breaded Prawns Tacos 29
Bacon-Wrapped Scallops 29
Tandoori Prawns...29
Sole and Cauliflower Fritters 30
Air Fried Spring Rolls 30
Fish Taco Bowl 30
Panko Catfish Nuggets 30
Bacon Halibut Steak 31
Lemony Salmon 31
Baked Grouper with Tomatoes and Garlic...........31
Tilapia Almondine 31
Classic Fish Sticks with Tartar Sauce 31

Cod Tacos with Mango Salsa 32
Fish Tacos with Jalapeño-Lime Sauce 32
Miso Salmon 32
Honey-Glazed Salmon 32
Baked Monkfish 33
Fish Cakes 33
Prawn Caesar Salad..33
Lemony Prawns...33
Sesame-Crusted Tuna Steak 34
Prawns Curry..34
Crab and Bell Pepper Cakes..............................34
Coconut Prawns 34

Chapter 5 Snacks and Appetizers 35

Sausage Balls with Cheese................................36
Crispy Cajun Fresh Dill Pickle Chips 36
Tortellini with Spicy Dipping Sauce 36
Cheesy Steak Fries 36
Crispy Mozzarella Cheese Sticks........................37
Peppery Chicken Meatballs................................37
Golden Onion Rings...37
Sweet Potato Fries with Mayonnaise 38
Caramelized Onion Dip with White Cheese..........38
String Bean Fries...38
Lebanese Muhammara 38
Spinach and Crab Meat Cups 39
Prawns Egg Rolls 39

Pork and Cabbage Egg Rolls..............................39
Kale Chips with Sesame.....................................40
Mushroom Tarts 40
Greens Chips with Curried Yoghurt Sauce 40
Cinnamon-Apple Crisps.....................................40
Parmesan Chips 41
Polenta Fries with Chilli-Lime Mayo 41
Stuffed Figs with Goat Cheese and Honey 41
Egg Roll Pizza Sticks...41
Easy Roasted Chickpeas 42
Old Bay Chicken Wings......................................42
Ranch Oyster Snack Crackers 42

Chapter 6 Family Favorites 43

Pecan Rolls..44
Fish and Vegetable Tacos 44
Berry Cheesecake...44
Mixed Berry Crumble 44
Pork Burgers with Red Cabbage Salad 45

Meringue Cookies 45
Old Bay Tilapia 45
Fried Green Tomatoes 45
Cheesy Roasted Sweet Potatoes........................46
Beef Jerky..46

Chapter 7 Fast and Easy Everyday Favourites

Cheesy Jalapeño Cornbread 48
Sweet Corn and Carrot Fritters 48
Baked Cheese Sandwich 48
Beetroot Salad with Lemon Vinaigrette 48
Bacon Pinwheels 49
Air Fried Broccoli 49
Cheesy Potato Patties 49
Air Fried Butternut Squash with Chopped Hazelnuts...........49

Rosemary and Orange Roasted Chickpeas 49
Simple Pea Delight...50
Scalloped Veggie Mix 50
Spinach and Carrot Balls...50
Traditional Queso Fundido.......................................50
Baked Chorizo Scotch Eggs.....................................50
Beef Bratwursts..51

Chapter 8 Vegetables and Sides

Crispy Lemon Artichoke Hearts...............................53
Spinach and Cheese Stuffed Tomatoes.......................53
Sweet and Crispy Roasted Pearl Onions.....................53
Cauliflower Rice Balls 53
Crispy Green Beans...54
Spiced Honey-Walnut Carrots 54
Indian Aubergine Bharta 54
Chermoula-Roasted Beetroots 54
Broccoli with Sesame Dressing 54
Southwestern Roasted Corn 55
Potato with Creamy Cheese 55
Flatbread...55
Parmesan-Rosemary Radishes 55

Courgette Fritters..55
Baked Jalapeño and Cheese Cauliflower Mash 56
Curried Fruit..56
Shishito Pepper Roast 56
Parmesan-Thyme Butternut Squash 56
Maple-Roasted Tomatoes.......................................56
Hasselback Potatoes with Chive Pesto......................57
Mashed Sweet Potato Tots 57
Fried Brussels Sprouts...57
Fried Asparagus...57
Turnip Fries 58
Tofu Bites 58

Chapter 9 Vegetarian Mains

Three-Cheese Courgette Boats................................60
Cauliflower Steak with Gremolata 60
Garlicky Sesame Carrots 60
Crustless Spinach Cheese Pie.................................60
Cheese Stuffed Peppers 61

Roasted Vegetable Mélange with Herbs..............................61
Super Veg Rolls...61
Super Vegetable Burger..61
Pesto Vegetable Skewers..61
Courgette and Spinach Croquettes............................62

Chapter 10 Desserts

Chickpea Brownies 64
Cream-Filled Sandwich Cookies...............................64
Gingerbread..64
Double Chocolate Brownies 64
Cream Cheese Shortbread Cookies...........................65
Pecan and Cherry Stuffed Apples.............................65
Roasted Honey Pears...65
Mini Peanut Butter Tarts 65

Chocolate Bread Pudding..66
Carrot Cake with Cream Cheese Icing........................66
Shortcut Spiced Apple Butter...................................66
Hazelnut Butter Cookies 66
Bourbon Bread Pudding...67
Luscious Coconut Pie..67
Dark Chocolate Lava Cake 67

Appendix Air Fryer Cooking Chart

INTRODUCTION

Are you tired of feeling guilty every time you indulge in your favorite fried foods? Do you dream of a world where crispy, golden fries and juicy chicken wings don't come with a side of guilt and regret? Well, my friend, I have some good news for you. The answer to your prayers comes in the form of a magical kitchen appliance known as the air fryer. Yes, you heard that right - an appliance that can fry up all your favorite foods using nothing but hot air! And if you're wondering how it's possible, well, let's just say it's like having a tiny tornado in your kitchen that whips up perfectly crispy and delicious meals without any of the oil or grease. So, get ready to say goodbye to soggy fries and hello to a healthier, happier you with this 2023 Easy Air Fryer Cookbook for Beginners UK.

Oh, let me tell you about my journey with the air fryer. It all started when I was browsing through a gourmet store and stumbled upon this sleek, futuristic-looking kitchen gadget. At first, I was skeptical - how could something that looked like a spaceship cook food? But being the adventurous foodie that I am, I decided to give it a try.

I brought the air fryer home and immediately started experimenting. The first thing I made was a batch of sweet potato fries, and let me tell you, they were a revelation. Perfectly crispy on the outside, soft and fluffy on the inside - and all without a drop of oil! I was hooked.

From there, I started trying out more and more recipes in the air fryer - everything from chicken wings to salmon to even donuts. And each time, I was blown away by how easy and convenient it was to use, not to mention how healthy and delicious the food turned out.

Now, I can't imagine my kitchen without my trusty air fryer by my side. It's become my go-to appliance for everything from quick weeknight dinners to impressive party snacks. And as a foodie, I'm always excited to discover new ways to use it and push its limits. Who knows what culinary adventures await me next with this magical machine?

To Know Your Air Fryer

An air fryer is a kitchen appliance that uses hot air to cook food, giving it a crispy and fried texture without the need for oil. It works by circulating hot air around the food at high speed, which cooks it evenly and quickly.

The air fryer has a heating element and a fan that circulates the hot air around the food. The food is placed in a basket or tray inside the air fryer, and the hot air is blown over and under the food, cooking it from all sides. Some air fryers also come with accessories like grills and racks that allow you to cook multiple items at once.

One of the main benefits of using an air fryer is that it can produce crispy and delicious results without the added fat and calories that come with traditional frying methods. It's also faster and more energy-efficient than using an oven, making it a great option for quick weeknight meals or snacks.

Overall, the air fryer is a versatile and convenient appliance that can help you create a wide range of tasty and healthy dishes with ease.

Why Air Frying?

Using an air fryer for cooking has several benefits, including:

1. Healthier meals: Air fryers use hot air to cook food, which means you don't need to use oil or other fats to get that crispy texture. This can help reduce the amount of fat and calories in your meals, making them healthier overall.

2. Faster cooking times: Air fryers heat up quickly and cook food faster than traditional ovens or stovetops. This can save you time and make it easier to get dinner on the table on busy weeknights.

3. Easy to use: Air fryers are simple to operate and require minimal prep work. Just place your food in the basket or tray, set the temperature and timer, and let the air fryer do the rest.

4. Versatile: Air fryers can cook a wide range of foods, from chicken wings to vegetables to desserts. Some models even come with accessories like grills and racks that allow you to cook multiple items at once.

5. Consistent results: Air fryers cook food evenly from all sides, which means you'll get consistent results every time. No more burnt edges or undercooked centers!

Overall, using an air fryer can help you create healthier, tastier meals with less effort and in less time. It's a versatile and convenient kitchen appliance that can help you take your cooking to the next level.

Here are some tips for using the air fryer effectively:

1. Preheat the air fryer: Just like with an oven, it's important to preheat your air fryer before cooking. This helps ensure even cooking and crispy results.

2. Don't overcrowd the basket: Make sure to leave some space between your food items in the basket or tray. Overcrowding can lead to uneven cooking and soggy results.

3. Shake the basket: To ensure even cooking, shake the basket or tray halfway through cooking to move the food around and expose all sides to the hot air.

4. Use a little oil: While you don't need to use oil to cook in an air fryer, using a little bit can help enhance the flavor and texture of your food. Try using a spray bottle to lightly coat your food with oil before cooking.

5. Experiment with different temperatures and times: Every air fryer is different, so it may take some trial and error to figure out the best temperature and cooking time for your favorite foods. Start with the recommended settings in your air fryer manual and adjust as needed.

6. Clean the air fryer regularly: To keep your air fryer working effectively, make sure to clean it regularly. Wipe down the basket and tray after each use, and deep clean the appliance as needed according to the manufacturer's instructions.

By following these tips, you can get the most out of your air fryer and create delicious, crispy meals every time.

Maintaining the Air Fryer

Maintaining an air fryer is important to ensure it continues to work effectively and produce delicious meals. Here are some tips for maintaining your air fryer:

1. Clean the basket and tray after each use: Wipe down the basket and tray with a damp cloth or sponge after each use to remove any food residue. Make sure they are completely dry before storing.

2. Deep clean the appliance regularly: Depending on how often you use your air fryer, you may need to deep clean it every few weeks or months. Check the manufacturer's instructions for specific cleaning recommendations.

3. Use non-abrasive cleaners: When cleaning your air fryer, avoid using abrasive cleaners or scrubbers that could scratch the surface. Instead, use a mild dish soap and a soft sponge or cloth.

4. Don't immerse the appliance in water: Air fryers are not designed to be submerged in water, so make sure to only clean the exterior and removable parts.

5. Store the appliance properly: When not in use, store your air fryer in a cool, dry place. Avoid stacking heavy objects on top of it or storing it near heat sources.

6. Replace damaged parts: If any parts of your air fryer become damaged or worn out, replace them as soon as possible. This can help prevent further damage and ensure the appliance continues to work effectively.

By following these maintenance tips, you can keep your air fryer in good condition and enjoy delicious, crispy meals for years to come.

Chapter 1 Breakfasts

Chapter 1 Breakfasts

Denver Omelette

Prep time: 5 minutes | Cook time: 8 minutes | Serves 1

2 large eggs
60 ml unsweetened, unflavoured almond milk
¼ teaspoon fine sea salt
⅛ teaspoon ground black pepper
60 g diced gammon (omit for vegetarian)
60 g diced green and red

peppers
2 tablespoons diced spring onions, plus more for garnish
60 g grated Cheddar cheese (about 30 g) (omit for dairy-free)
Quartered cherry tomatoes, for serving (optional)

1. Preheat the air fryer to 180°C. Grease a cake pan and set aside. 2. In a small bowl, use a fork to whisk together the eggs, almond milk, salt, and pepper. Add the ham, peppers, and spring onions. Pour the mixture into the greased pan. Add the cheese on top (if using). 3. Place the pan in the basket of the air fryer. Bake for 8 minutes, or until the eggs are cooked to your liking. 4. Loosen the omelette from the sides of the pan with a spatula and place it on a serving plate. Garnish with spring onions and serve with cherry tomatoes, if desired. Best served fresh.

Keto Quiche

Prep time: 10 minutes | Cook time: 1 hour | Makes 1 (6-inch) quiche

Crust:
150 g blanched almond flour
300 g grated Parmesan or Gouda cheese
¼ teaspoon fine sea salt
1 large egg, beaten
Filling:
120 g chicken or beef stock (or vegetable stock for vegetarian)
235 g grated Swiss cheese (about 110 g)

110 g soft cheese (120 ml)
1 tablespoon unsalted butter, melted
4 large eggs, beaten
80 g minced leeks or sliced spring onions
¾ teaspoon fine sea salt
⅛ teaspoon cayenne pepper
Chopped spring onions, for garnish

1. Preheat the air fryer to 160°C. Grease a pie pan. Spray two large pieces of parchment paper with avocado oil and set them on the countertop. 2. Make the crust: In a medium-sized bowl, combine the flour, cheese, and salt and mix well. Add the egg and mix until the dough is well combined and stiff. 3. Place the dough in the center of one of the greased pieces of parchment. Top with the other piece of parchment. Using a rolling pin, roll out the dough into a circle about 1/16 inch thick. 4. Press the pie crust into the prepared pie pan. Place it in the air fryer and bake for 12 minutes, or until it starts to lightly brown. 5. While the crust bakes, make the filling: In a large bowl, combine the stock, Swiss cheese, soft cheese, and butter. Stir in the eggs, leeks, salt, and cayenne pepper. When the crust is ready, pour the mixture into the crust. 6. Place the quiche in the air fryer and bake for 15 minutes. Turn the heat down to 150°C and bake for an additional 30 minutes, or until a knife inserted 1 inch from the edge comes out clean. You may have to cover the edges of the crust with foil to prevent burning. 7. Allow the quiche to cool for 10 minutes before garnishing it with chopped spring onions and cutting it into wedges. 8. Store leftovers in an airtight container in the refrigerator for up to 4 days or in the freezer for up to a month. Reheat in a preheated 180°C air fryer for a few minutes, until warmed through.

Bourbon Vanilla French Toast

Prep time: 15 minutes | Cook time: 6 minutes | Serves 4

2 large eggs
2 tablespoons water
160 ml whole or semi-skimmed milk
1 tablespoon butter, melted

2 tablespoons bourbon
1 teaspoon vanilla extract
8 (1-inch-thick) French bread slices
Cooking spray

1. Preheat the air fryer to 160°C. Line the air fryer basket with parchment paper and spray it with cooking spray. 2. Beat the eggs with the water in a shallow bowl until combined. Add the milk, melted butter, bourbon, and vanilla and stir to mix well. 3. Dredge 4 slices of bread in the batter, turning to coat both sides evenly. Transfer the bread slices onto the parchment paper. 4. Bake for 6 minutes until nicely browned. Flip the slices halfway through the cooking time. 5. Remove from the basket to a plate and repeat with the remaining 4 slices of bread. 6. Serve warm.

Sausage and Egg Breakfast Burrito

Prep time: 5 minutes | Cook time: 30 minutes |
Serves 6

6 eggs
Salt and pepper, to taste
Cooking oil
120 g chopped red pepper
120 g chopped green pepper
230 g chicken sausage meat

(removed from casings)
120 ml tomato salsa
6 medium (8-inch) wheat
tortillas
120 g grated Cheddar cheese

1. In a medium bowl, whisk the eggs. Add salt and pepper to taste. 2. Place a skillet on medium-high heat. Spray with cooking oil. Add the eggs. Scramble for 2 to 3 minutes, until the eggs are fluffy. Remove the eggs from the skillet and set aside. 3. If needed, spray the skillet with more oil. Add the chopped red and green bell peppers. Cook for 2 to 3 minutes, until the peppers are soft. 4. Add the sausage meat to the skillet. Break the sausage into smaller pieces using a spatula or spoon. Cook for 3 to 4 minutes, until the sausage is brown. 5. Add the tomato salsa and scrambled eggs. Stir to combine. Remove the skillet from heat. 6. Spoon the mixture evenly onto the tortillas. 7. To form the burritos, fold the sides of each tortilla in toward the middle and then roll up from the bottom. You can secure each burrito with a toothpick. Or you can moisten the outside edge of the tortilla with a small amount of water. I prefer to use a cooking brush, but you can also dab with your fingers. 8. Spray the burritos with cooking oil and place them in the air fryer. Do not stack. Cook the burritos in batches if they do not all fit in the basket. Air fry at 200ºC for 8 minutes. 9. Open the air fryer and flip the burritos. Cook for an additional 2 minutes or until crisp. 10. If necessary, repeat steps 8 and 9 for the remaining burritos. 11. Sprinkle the Cheddar cheese over the burritos. Cool before serving.

Cheddar Soufflés

Prep time: 15 minutes | Cook time: 12 minutes |
Serves 4

3 large eggs, whites and yolks
separated
¼ teaspoon cream of tartar

120 g grated mature Cheddar
cheese
85 g soft cheese, softened

1. In a large bowl, beat egg whites together with cream of tartar until soft peaks form, about 2 minutes. 2. In a separate medium bowl, beat egg yolks, Cheddar, and soft cheese together until frothy, about 1 minute. Add egg yolk mixture to whites, gently folding until combined. 3. Pour mixture evenly into four ramekins greased with cooking spray. Place ramekins into air fryer basket. Adjust the temperature to 180ºC and bake for 12 minutes. Eggs will be browned on the top and firm in the center when done. Serve warm.

Pancake Cake

Prep time: 10 minutes | Cook time: 7 minutes |
Serves 4

60 g blanched finely ground
almond flour
30 g powdered erythritol
½ teaspoon baking powder
2 tablespoons unsalted butter,

softened
1 large egg
½ teaspoon unflavoured gelatin
½ teaspoon vanilla extract
½ teaspoon ground cinnamon

1. In a large bowl, mix almond flour, erythritol, and baking powder. Add butter, egg, gelatin, vanilla, and cinnamon. Pour into a round baking pan. 2. Place pan into the air fryer basket. 3. Adjust the temperature to 150ºC and set the timer for 7 minutes. 4. When the cake is completely cooked, a toothpick will come out clean. Cut cake into four and serve.

Gyro Breakfast Patties with Tzatziki

Prep time: 10 minutes | Cook time: 20 minutes per
batch | Makes 16

Patties:
900 g lamb or beef mince
120 g diced red onions
60 g sliced black olives
2 tablespoons tomato sauce
1 teaspoon dried oregano leaves
2 cloves garlic, minced
1 teaspoon fine sea salt
Tzatziki:
235 ml full-fat sour cream
1 small cucumber, chopped
½ teaspoon fine sea salt

½ teaspoon garlic powder, or 1
clove garlic, minced
¼ teaspoon dried dill, or 1
teaspoon finely chopped fresh
dill
For Garnish/Serving:
120 g crumbled feta cheese
(about 60 g)
Diced red onions
Sliced black olives
Sliced cucumbers

1. Preheat the air fryer to 180ºC. 2. Place the lamb, onions, olives, tomato sauce, oregano, garlic, and salt in a large bowl. Mix well to combine the ingredients. 3. Using your hands, form the mixture into sixteen 3-inch patties. Place about 5 of the patties in the air fryer and air fry for 20 minutes, flipping halfway through. Remove the patties and place them on a serving platter. Repeat with the remaining patties. 4. While the patties cook, make the tzatziki: Place all the ingredients in a small bowl and stir well. Cover and store in the fridge until ready to serve. Garnish with ground black pepper before serving. 5. Serve the patties with a dollop of tzatziki, a sprinkle of crumbled feta cheese, diced red onions, sliced black olives, and sliced cucumbers. 6. Store leftovers in an airtight container in the refrigerator for up to 5 days or in the freezer for up to a month. Reheat the patties in a preheated 200ºC air fryer for a few minutes, until warmed through.

Simple Cinnamon Toasts

Prep time: 5 minutes | Cook time: 4 minutes | Serves 4

1 tablespoon salted butter	½ teaspoon vanilla extract
2 teaspoons ground cinnamon	10 bread slices
4 tablespoons sugar	

1. Preheat the air fryer to 190ºC. 2. In a bowl, combine the butter, cinnamon, sugar, and vanilla extract. Spread onto the slices of bread. 3. Put the bread inside the air fryer and bake for 4 minutes or until golden brown. 4. Serve warm.

Veggie Frittata

Prep time: 7 minutes | Cook time: 21 to 23 minutes | Serves 2

Avocado oil spray	85 g grated mature Cheddar cheese, divided
60 g diced red onion	
60 g diced red pepper	½ teaspoon dried thyme
60 g finely chopped broccoli	Sea salt and freshly ground black pepper, to taste
4 large eggs	

1. Spray a pan well with oil. Put the onion, pepper, and broccoli in the pan, place the pan in the air fryer, and set to 180ºC. Bake for 5 minutes. 2. While the vegetables cook, beat the eggs in a medium bowl. Stir in half of the cheese, and season with the thyme, salt, and pepper. 3. Add the eggs to the pan and top with the remaining cheese. Set the air fryer to 180ºC. Bake for 16 to 18 minutes, until cooked through.

Pancake for Two

Prep time: 5 minutes | Cook time: 30 minutes | Serves 2

120 g blanched finely ground almond flour	melted
	1 large egg
2 tablespoons granular erythritol	80 ml unsweetened almond milk
1 tablespoon salted butter,	½ teaspoon vanilla extract

1. In a large bowl, mix all ingredients together, then pour half the batter into an ungreased round nonstick baking dish. 2. Place dish into air fryer basket. Adjust the temperature to 160ºC and bake for 15 minutes. The pancake will be golden brown on top and firm, and a toothpick inserted in the center will come out clean when done. Repeat with remaining batter. 3. Slice in half in dish and serve warm.

Nutty Granola

Prep time: 5 minutes | Cook time: 1 hour | Serves 4

120 g pecans, roughly chopped	2 tablespoons melted butter
120 g walnuts or almonds, roughly chopped	60 ml granulated sweetener
	½ teaspoon ground cinnamon
60 g desiccated coconut	½ teaspoon vanilla extract
30 g almond flour	¼ teaspoon ground nutmeg
60 g ground flaxseed or chia seeds	¼ teaspoon salt
	2 tablespoons water
2 tablespoons sunflower seeds	

1. Preheat the air fryer to 120ºC. Cut a piece of parchment paper to fit inside the air fryer basket. 2. In a large bowl, toss the nuts, coconut, almond flour, ground flaxseed or chia seeds, sunflower seeds, butter, sweetener, cinnamon, vanilla, nutmeg, salt, and water until thoroughly combined. 3. Spread the granola on the parchment paper and flatten to an even thickness. 4. Air fry for about an hour, or until golden throughout. Remove from the air fryer and allow to fully cool. Break the granola into bite-size pieces and store in a covered container for up to a week.

Mushroom-and-Tomato Stuffed Hash Browns

Prep time: 10 minutes | Cook time: 20 minutes | Serves 4

rapeseed oil cooking spray	1 garlic clove, minced
1 tablespoon plus 2 teaspoons rapeseed oil, divided	475 g grated potatoes
	½ teaspoon salt
110 g baby mushrooms, diced	¼ teaspoon black pepper
1 spring onion, white parts and green parts, diced	1 plum tomato, diced
	120 g grated mozzarella

1. Preheat the air fryer to 190ºC. Lightly coat the inside of a 6-inch cake pan with rapeseed oil cooking spray. 2. In a small skillet, heat 2 teaspoons rapeseed oil over medium heat. Add the mushrooms, spring onion, and garlic, and cook for 4 to 5 minutes, or until they have softened and are beginning to show some color. Remove from heat. 3. Meanwhile, in a large bowl, combine the potatoes, salt, pepper, and the remaining tablespoon rapeseed oil. Toss until all potatoes are well coated. 4. Pour half of the potatoes into the bottom of the cake pan. Top with the mushroom mixture, tomato, and mozzarella. Spread the remaining potatoes over the top. 5. Bake in the air fryer for 12 to 15 minutes, or until the top is golden brown. 6. Remove from the air fryer and allow to cool for 5 minutes before slicing and serving.

Sausage Stuffed Peppers

Prep time: 15 minutes | Cook time: 15 minutes |
Serves 4

230 g spicy pork sausage meat, removed from casings
4 large eggs
110 g full-fat soft cheese, softened
60 g tinned diced tomatoes,

drained
4 green peppers
8 tablespoons grated chilli cheese
120 ml full-fat sour cream

1. In a medium skillet over medium heat, crumble and brown the sausage meat until no pink remains. Remove sausage and drain the fat from the pan. Crack eggs into the pan, scramble, and cook until no longer runny. 2. Place cooked sausage in a large bowl and fold in soft cheese. Mix in diced tomatoes. Gently fold in eggs. 3. Cut a 4-inch to 5-inch slit in the top of each pepper, removing the seeds and white membrane with a small knife. Separate the filling into four servings and spoon carefully into each pepper. Top each with 2 tablespoons cheese. 4. Place each pepper into the air fryer basket. 5. Adjust the temperature to 180°C and set the timer for 15 minutes. 6. Peppers will be soft and cheese will be browned when ready. Serve immediately with sour cream on top.

Fried Chicken Wings with Waffles

Prep time: 10 minutes | Cook time: 30 minutes |
Serves 4

8 whole chicken wings
1 teaspoon garlic powder
Chicken seasoning, for preparing the chicken
Freshly ground black pepper, to taste

60 g plain flour
Cooking oil spray
8 frozen waffles
Pure maple syrup, for serving (optional)

1. In a medium bowl, combine the chicken and garlic powder and season with chicken seasoning and pepper. Toss to coat. 2. Transfer the chicken to a resealable plastic bag and add the flour. Seal the bag and shake it to coat the chicken thoroughly. 3. Insert the crisper plate into the basket and the basket into the unit. Preheat the unit by selecting AIR FRY, setting the temperature to 200°C, and setting the time to 3 minutes. Select START/STOP to begin. 4. Once the unit is preheated, spray the crisper plate with cooking oil. Using tongs, transfer the chicken from the bag to the basket. It is okay to stack the chicken wings on top of each other. Spray them with cooking oil. 5. Select AIR FRY, set the temperature to 200°C, and set the time to 20 minutes. Select START/STOP to begin. 6. After 5 minutes, remove the basket and shake the wings. Reinsert the basket to resume cooking. Remove and shake the basket every 5

minutes until the chicken is fully cooked. 7. When the cooking is complete, remove the cooked chicken from the basket; cover to keep warm. 8. Rinse the basket and crisper plate with warm water. Insert them back into the unit. 9. Select AIR FRY, set the temperature to 180°C, and set the time to 3 minutes. Select START/STOP to begin. 10. Once the unit is preheated, spray the crisper plate with cooking spray. Working in batches, place the frozen waffles into the basket. Do not stack them. Spray the waffles with cooking oil. 11. Select AIR FRY, set the temperature to 180°C, and set the time to 6 minutes. Select START/STOP to begin. 12. When the cooking is complete, repeat steps 10 and 11 with the remaining waffles. 13. Serve the waffles with the chicken and a touch of maple syrup, if desired.

Poached Eggs on Whole Grain Avocado Toast

Prep time: 5 minutes | Cook time: 7 minutes | Serves 4

rapeseed oil cooking spray
4 large eggs
Salt
Black pepper

4 pieces wholegrain bread
1 avocado
Red pepper flakes (optional)

1. Preheat the air fryer to 160°C. Lightly coat the inside of four small oven-safe ramekins with rapeseed oil cooking spray. 2. Crack one egg into each ramekin, and season with salt and black pepper. 3. Place the ramekins into the air fryer basket. Close and set the timer to 7 minutes. 4. While the eggs are cooking, toast the bread in a toaster. 5. Slice the avocado in half lengthwise, remove the pit, and scoop the flesh into a small bowl. Season with salt, black pepper, and red pepper flakes, if desired. Using a fork, smash the avocado lightly. 6. Spread a quarter of the smashed avocado evenly over each slice of toast. 7. Remove the eggs from the air fryer, and gently spoon one onto each slice of avocado toast before serving.

Canadian Bacon Muffin Sandwiches

Prep time: 5 minutes | Cook time: 8 minutes | Serves 4

4 muffins, split
8 slices back bacon

4 slices cheese
Cooking spray

1. Preheat the air fryer to 190°C. 2. Make the sandwiches: Top each of 4 muffin halves with 2 slices of bacon, 1 slice of cheese, and finish with the remaining muffin half. 3. Put the sandwiches in the air fryer basket and spritz the tops with cooking spray. 4. Bake for 4 minutes. Flip the sandwiches and bake for another 4 minutes. 5. Divide the sandwiches among four plates and serve warm.

Butternut Squash and Ricotta Frittata

Prep time: 10 minutes | Cook time: 33 minutes | Serves 2 to 3

235 ml cubed (½-inch) butternut squash (160 g)
2 tablespoons rapeseed oil
Coarse or flaky salt and freshly ground black pepper, to taste
4 fresh sage leaves, thinly sliced
6 large eggs, lightly beaten
120 g ricotta cheese
Cayenne pepper

1. In a bowl, toss the squash with the rapeseed oil and season with salt and black pepper until evenly coated. Sprinkle the sage on the bottom of a cake pan and place the squash on top. Place the pan in the air fryer and bake at 200ºC for 10 minutes. Stir to incorporate the sage, then cook until the squash is tender and lightly caramelized at the edges, about 3 minutes more. 2. Pour the eggs over the squash, dollop the ricotta all over, and sprinkle with cayenne. Bake at 150ºC until the eggs are set and the frittata is golden brown on top, about 20 minutes. Remove the pan from the air fryer and cut the frittata into wedges to serve.

Honey-Apricot Granola with Greek Yoghurt

Prep time: 10 minutes | Cook time: 30 minutes | Serves 6

235 g porridge oats
60 g dried apricots, diced
60 g almond slivers
60 g walnuts, chopped
60 g pumpkin seeds
60 to 80 ml honey, plus more for drizzling
1 tablespoon rapeseed oil
1 teaspoon ground cinnamon
¼ teaspoon ground nutmeg
¼ teaspoon salt
2 tablespoons sugar-free dark chocolate chips (optional)
700 ml fat-free natural yoghurt

1. Preheat the air fryer to 130ºC. Line the air fryer basket with parchment paper. 2. In a large bowl, combine the oats, apricots, almonds, walnuts, pumpkin seeds, honey, rapeseed oil, cinnamon, nutmeg, and salt, mixing so that the honey, oil, and spices are well distributed. 3. Pour the mixture onto the parchment paper and spread it into an even layer. 4. Bake for 10 minutes, then shake or stir and spread back out into an even layer. Continue baking for 10 minutes more, then repeat the process of shaking or stirring the mixture. Bake for an additional 10 minutes before removing from the air fryer. 5. Allow the granola to cool completely before stirring in the chocolate chips (if using) and pouring into an airtight container for storage. 6. For each serving, top 120 ml Greek yoghurt with 80 ml granola and a drizzle of honey, if needed.

Smoky Sausage Patties

Prep time: 30 minutes | Cook time: 9 minutes | Serves 8

450 g pork mince
1 tablespoon soy sauce or tamari
1 teaspoon smoked paprika
1 teaspoon dried sage
1 teaspoon sea salt
½ teaspoon fennel seeds
½ teaspoon dried thyme
½ teaspoon freshly ground black pepper
¼ teaspoon cayenne pepper

1. In a large bowl, combine the pork, soy sauce, smoked paprika, sage, salt, fennel seeds, thyme, black pepper, and cayenne pepper. Work the meat with your hands until the seasonings are fully incorporated. 2. Shape the mixture into 8 equal-size patties. Using your thumb, make a dent in the center of each patty. Place the patties on a plate and cover with plastic wrap. Refrigerate the patties for at least 30 minutes. 3. Working in batches if necessary, place the patties in a single layer in the air fryer, being careful not to overcrowd them. 4. Set the air fryer to 200ºC and air fry for 5 minutes. Flip and cook for about 4 minutes more.

All-in-One Toast

Prep time: 10 minutes | Cook time: 10 minutes | Serves 1

1 strip bacon, diced
1 slice 1-inch thick bread
1 egg
Salt and freshly ground black
pepper, to taste
60 g grated Monterey Jack or Chedday cheese

1. Preheat the air fryer to 200ºC. 2. Air fry the bacon for 3 minutes, shaking the basket once or twice while it cooks. Remove the bacon to a paper towel lined plate and set aside. 3. Use a sharp paring knife to score a large circle in the middle of the slice of bread, cutting halfway through, but not all the way through to the cutting board. Press down on the circle in the center of the bread slice to create an indentation. 4. Transfer the slice of bread, hole side up, to the air fryer basket. Crack the egg into the center of the bread, and season with salt and pepper. 5. Adjust the air fryer temperature to 190ºC and air fry for 5 minutes. Sprinkle the grated cheese around the edges of the bread, leaving the center of the yolk uncovered, and top with the cooked bacon. Press the cheese and bacon into the bread lightly to help anchor it to the bread and prevent it from blowing around in the air fryer. 6. Air fry for one or two more minutes, just to melt the cheese and finish cooking the egg. Serve immediately.

Spinach and Bacon Roll-ups

Prep time: 5 minutes | Cook time: 8 to 9 minutes | Serves 4

4 wheat tortillas (6 or 7-inch size)
4 slices Swiss cheese
235 g baby spinach leaves

4 slices turkey bacon
Special Equipment:
4 cocktail sticks, soak in water for at least 30 minutes

1. Preheat the air fryer to 200ºC. 2. On a clean work surface, top each tortilla with one slice of cheese and 60 ml spinach, then tightly roll them up. 3. Wrap each tortilla with a strip of turkey bacon and secure with a toothpick. 4. Arrange the roll-ups in the air fryer basket, leaving space between each roll-up. 5. Air fry for 4 minutes. Flip the roll-ups with tongs and rearrange them for more even cooking. Air fry for another 4 to 5 minutes until the bacon is crisp. 6. Rest for 5 minutes and remove the cocktail sticks before serving.

Parmesan Sausage Egg Muffins

Prep time: 5 minutes | Cook time: 20 minutes | Serves 4

170 g Italian-seasoned sausage, sliced
6 eggs
30 ml double cream

Salt and ground black pepper, to taste
85 g Parmesan cheese, grated

1. Preheat the air fryer to 180ºC. Grease a muffin pan. 2. Put the sliced sausage in the muffin pan. 3. Beat the eggs with the cream in a bowl and season with salt and pepper. 4. Pour half of the mixture over the sausages in the pan. 5. Sprinkle with cheese and the remaining egg mixture. 6. Bake in the preheated air fryer for 20 minutes or until set. 7. Serve immediately.

Bacon, Cheese, and Avocado Melt

Prep time: 5 minutes | Cook time: 3 to 5 minutes | Serves 2

1 avocado
4 slices cooked bacon, chopped
2 tablespoons tomato salsa

1 tablespoon double cream
60 g grated Cheddar cheese

1. Preheat the air fryer to 200ºC. 2. Slice the avocado in half lengthwise and remove the stone. To ensure the avocado halves do not roll in the basket, slice a thin piece of skin off the base. 3. In a small bowl, combine the bacon, tomato salsa, and cream. Divide the mixture between the avocado halves and top with the cheese. 4.

Place the avocado halves in the air fryer basket and air fry for 3 to 5 minutes until the cheese has melted and begins to brown. Serve warm.

Meritage Eggs

Prep time: 5 minutes | Cook time: 8 minutes | Serves 2

2 teaspoons unsalted butter (or coconut oil for dairy-free), for greasing the ramekins
4 large eggs
2 teaspoons chopped fresh thyme
½ teaspoon fine sea salt
¼ teaspoon ground black pepper

2 tablespoons double cream (or unsweetened, unflavoured almond milk for dairy-free)
3 tablespoons finely grated Parmesan cheese (or chive soft cheese style spread, softened, for dairy-free)
Fresh thyme leaves, for garnish (optional)

1. Preheat the air fryer to 200ºC. Grease two (110 g) ramekins with the butter. 2. Crack 2 eggs into each ramekin and divide the thyme, salt, and pepper between the ramekins. Pour 1 tablespoon of the heavy cream into each ramekin. Sprinkle each ramekin with 1½ tablespoons of the Parmesan cheese. 3. Place the ramekins in the air fryer and bake for 8 minutes for soft-cooked yolks (longer if you desire a harder yolk). 4. Garnish with a sprinkle of ground black pepper and thyme leaves, if desired. Best served fresh.

Baked Peach Oatmeal

Prep time: 5 minutes | Cook time: 30 minutes | Serves 6

rapeseed oil cooking spray
475 g certified gluten-free porridge oats
475 ml unsweetened almond milk
60 ml honey, plus more for drizzling (optional)

120 ml non-fat natural yoghurt
1 teaspoon vanilla extract
½ teaspoon ground cinnamon
¼ teaspoon salt
350 g diced peaches, divided, plus more for serving (optional)

1. Preheat the air fryer to 190ºC. Lightly coat the inside of a 6-inch cake pan with rapeseed oil cooking spray. 2. In a large bowl, mix together the oats, almond milk, honey, yoghurt, vanilla, cinnamon, and salt until well combined. 3. Fold in 180 g peaches and then pour the mixture into the prepared cake pan. 4. Sprinkle the remaining peaches across the top of the oatmeal mixture. Bake in the air fryer for 30 minutes. 5. Allow to set and cool for 5 minutes before serving with additional fresh fruit and honey for drizzling, if desired.

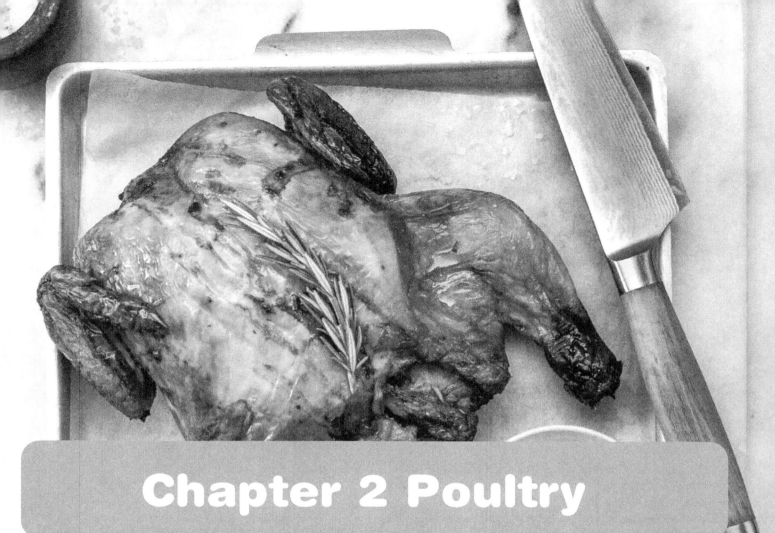

Chapter 2 Poultry

Chicken Schnitzel Dogs

Prep time: 15 minutes | Cook time: 8 to 10 minutes | Serves 4

30 g flour	4 chicken tenders, pounded thin
½ teaspoon salt	Oil for misting or cooking spray
1 teaspoon marjoram	4 whole-grain hotdog buns
1 teaspoon dried parsley flakes	4 slices Gouda cheese
½ teaspoon thyme	1 small Granny Smith apple,
1 egg	thinly sliced
1 teaspoon lemon juice	45 g shredded Swiss Chard
1 teaspoon water	cabbage
60 g bread crumbs	Coleslaw dressing

1. In a shallow dish, mix together the flour, salt, marjoram, parsley, and thyme. 2. In another shallow dish, beat together egg, lemon juice, and water. 3. Place bread crumbs in a third shallow dish. 4. Cut each of the flattened chicken tenders in half lengthwise. 5. Dip flattened chicken strips in flour mixture, then egg wash. Let excess egg drip off and roll in bread crumbs. Spray both sides with oil or cooking spray. 6. Air fry at 200ºC for 5 minutes. Spray with oil, turn over, and spray other side. 7. Cook for 3 to 5 minutes more, until well done and crispy brown. 8. To serve, place 2 schnitzel strips on bottom of each hotdog bun. Top with cheese, sliced apple, and cabbage. Drizzle with coleslaw dressing and top with other half of bun.

Greek Chicken Souvlaki

Prep time: 30 minutes | Cook time: 15 minutes | Serves 3 to 4

Chicken:	Vegetable oil spray
Grated zest and juice of 1	For Serving:
lemon	Warm pita bread or hot cooked
2 tablespoons extra-virgin olive	rice
oil	Sliced ripe tomatoes
1 tablespoon Greek souvlaki	Sliced cucumbers
seasoning	Thinly sliced red onion
450 g boneless, skinless chicken	Kalamata olives
breast, cut into 2-inch chunks	Tzatziki

1. For the chicken: In a small bowl, combine the lemon zest,

lemon juice, olive oil, and souvlaki seasoning. Place the chicken in a gallon-size resealable plastic bag. Pour the marinade over chicken. Seal bag and massage to coat. Place the bag in a large bowl and marinate for 30 minutes, or cover and refrigerate up to 24 hours, turning the bag occasionally. 2. Place the chicken a single layer in the air fryer basket. Set the air fryer to 180ºC for 10 minutes, turning the chicken and spraying with a little vegetable oil spray halfway through the cooking time. Increase the air fryer temperature to 200ºC for 5 minutes to allow the chicken to crisp and brown a little. 3. Transfer the chicken to a serving platter and serve with pita bread or rice, tomatoes, cucumbers, onion, olives and tzatziki.

Crunchy Chicken with Roasted Carrots

Prep time: 10 minutes | Cook time: 22 minutes | Serves 4

4 bone-in, skin-on chicken	1 teaspoon sea salt, divided
thighs	2 teaspoons chopped fresh
2 carrots, cut into 2-inch pieces	rosemary leaves
2 tablespoons extra-virgin olive	Cooking oil spray
oil	500 g cooked white rice
2 teaspoons poultry spice	

1. Brush the chicken thighs and carrots with olive oil. Sprinkle both with the poultry spice, salt, and rosemary. 2. Insert the crisper plate into the basket and the basket into the unit. Preheat the unit by selecting AIR FRY, setting the temperature to 200ºC, and setting the time to 3 minutes. Select START/STOP to begin. 3. Once the unit is preheated, spray the crisper plate with cooking oil. Place the carrots into the basket. Add the wire rack and arrange the chicken thighs on the rack. 4. Select AIR FRY, set the temperature to 200ºC, and set the time to 20 minutes. Select START/STOP to begin. 5. When the cooking is complete, check the chicken temperature. If a food thermometer inserted into the chicken registers 76ºC, remove the chicken from the air fryer, place it on a clean plate, and cover with aluminum foil to keep warm. Otherwise, resume cooking for 1 to 2 minutes longer. 6. The carrots can cook for 18 to 22 minutes and will be tender and caramelized; cooking time isn't as crucial for root vegetables. 7. Serve the chicken and carrots with the hot cooked rice.

Chipotle Aioli Wings

Prep time: 5 minutes | Cook time: 25 minutes | Serves 6

900 g bone-in chicken wings	2 tablespoons mayonnaise
½ teaspoon salt	2 teaspoons chipotle powder
¼ teaspoon ground black pepper	2 tablespoons lemon juice

1. In a large bowl, toss wings in salt and pepper, then place into ungreased air fryer basket. Adjust the temperature to 200ºC and air fry for 25 minutes, shaking the basket twice while cooking. Wings will be done when golden and have an internal temperature of at least 76ºC. 2. In a small bowl, whisk together mayonnaise, chipotle powder, and lemon juice. Place cooked wings into a large serving bowl and drizzle with aioli. Toss to coat. Serve warm.

Teriyaki Chicken Legs

Prep time: 12 minutes | Cook time: 18 to 20 minutes | Serves 2

4 tablespoons teriyaki sauce	4 chicken legs
1 tablespoon orange juice	Cooking spray
1 teaspoon smoked paprika	

1. Mix together the teriyaki sauce, orange juice, and smoked paprika. Brush on all sides of chicken legs. 2. Spray the air fryer basket with nonstick cooking spray and place chicken in basket. 3. Air fry at 180ºC for 6 minutes. Turn and baste with sauce. Cook for 6 more minutes, turn and baste. Cook for 6 to 8 minutes more, until juices run clear when chicken is pierced with a fork.

Chicken Nuggets

Prep time: 10 minutes | Cook time: 15 minutes | Serves 4

450 g chicken mince thighs	½ teaspoon salt
110 g shredded Mozzarella cheese	¼ teaspoon dried oregano
1 large egg, whisked	¼ teaspoon garlic powder

1. In a large bowl, combine all ingredients. Form mixture into twenty nugget shapes, about 2 tablespoons each. 2. Place nuggets into ungreased air fryer basket, working in batches if needed. Adjust the temperature to (190ºC and air fry for 15 minutes, turning nuggets halfway through cooking. Let cool 5 minutes before serving.

Chicken Wellington

Prep time: 30 minutes | Cook time: 31 minutes | Serves 2

2 (140 g) boneless, skinless chicken breasts	2 tablespoons White Worcestershire sauce (or white wine)
120 ml White Worcestershire sauce	Salt and freshly ground black pepper, to taste
3 tablespoons butter	1 tablespoon chopped fresh tarragon
25 g finely diced onion (about ½ onion)	2 sheets puff pastry, thawed
225 g button mushrooms, finely chopped	1 egg, beaten
60 ml chicken stock	Vegetable oil

1. Place the chicken breasts in a shallow dish. Pour the White Worcestershire sauce over the chicken coating both sides and marinate for 30 minutes. 2. While the chicken is marinating, melt the butter in a large skillet over medium-high heat on the stovetop. Add the onion and sauté for a few minutes, until it starts to soften. Add the mushrooms and sauté for 3 to 5 minutes until the vegetables are brown and soft. Deglaze the skillet with the chicken stock, scraping up any bits from the bottom of the pan. Add the White Worcestershire sauce and simmer for 2 to 3 minutes until the mixture reduces and starts to thicken. Season with salt and freshly ground black pepper. Remove the mushroom mixture from the heat and stir in the fresh tarragon. Let the mushroom mixture cool. 3. Preheat the air fryer to 180ºC. 4. Remove the chicken from the marinade and transfer it to the air fryer basket. Tuck the small end of the chicken breast under the thicker part to shape it into a circle rather than an oval. Pour the marinade over the chicken and air fry for 10 minutes. 5. Roll out the puff pastry and cut out two 6-inch squares. Brush the perimeter of each square with the egg wash. Place half of the mushroom mixture in the centre of each puff pastry square. Place the chicken breasts, top side down on the mushroom mixture. Starting with one corner of puff pastry and working in one direction, pull the pastry up over the chicken to enclose it and press the ends of the pastry together in the middle. Brush the pastry with the egg wash to seal the edges. Turn the Wellingtons over and set aside. 6. Make a decorative design with the remaining puff pastry, cut out four 10-inch strips. For each Wellington, twist two of the strips together, place them over the chicken breast wrapped in puff pastry, and tuck the ends underneath to seal it. Brush the entire top and sides of the Wellingtons with the egg wash. 7. Preheat the air fryer to 180ºC. . 8. Spray or brush the air fryer basket with vegetable oil. Air fry the chicken Wellingtons for 13 minutes. Carefully turn the Wellingtons over. Air fry for another 8 minutes. Transfer to serving plates, light a candle and enjoy!

Golden Tenders

60 g panko bread crumbs
1 tablespoon paprika
½ teaspoon salt
¼ teaspoon freshly ground

black pepper
16 chicken tenders
115 g mayonnaise
Olive oil spray

1. In a medium bowl, stir together the panko, paprika, salt, and pepper. 2. In a large bowl, toss together the chicken tenders and mayonnaise to coat. Transfer the coated chicken pieces to the bowl of seasoned panko and dredge to coat thoroughly. Press the coating onto the chicken with your fingers. 3. Insert the crisper plate into the basket and the basket into the unit. Preheat the unit by selecting AIR FRY, setting the temperature to 180°C, and setting the time to 3 minutes. Select START/STOP to begin. 4. Once the unit is preheated, place a parchment paper liner into the basket. Place the chicken into the basket and spray it with olive oil. 5. Select AIR FRY, set the temperature to 180°C, and set the time to 15 minutes. Select START/STOP to begin. 6. When the cooking is complete, the tenders will be golden brown and a food thermometer inserted into the chicken should register 76°C. For more even browning, remove the basket halfway through cooking and flip the tenders. Give them an extra spray of olive oil and reinsert the basket to resume cooking. This ensures they are crispy and brown all over. 7. When the cooking is complete, serve.

Apricot-Glazed Turkey Tenderloin

Olive oil
80 g sugar-free apricot preserves
½ tablespoon spicy brown

mustard
680 g turkey breast tenderloin
Salt and freshly ground black pepper, to taste

1. Spray the air fryer basket lightly with olive oil. 2. In a small bowl, combine the apricot preserves and mustard to make a paste. 3. Season the turkey with salt and pepper. Spread the apricot paste all over the turkey. 4. Place the turkey in the air fryer basket and lightly spray with olive oil. 5. Air fry at 190°C for 15 minutes. Flip the turkey over and lightly spray with olive oil. Air fry until the internal temperature reaches at least 80°C, an additional 10 to 15 minutes. 6. Let the turkey rest for 10 minutes before slicing and serving.

Sweet and Spicy Turkey Meatballs

Olive oil
450 g lean turkey mince
30 g whole-wheat panko bread crumbs
1 egg, beaten
1 tablespoon soy sauce
60 ml plus 1 tablespoon hoisin

sauce, divided
2 teaspoons minced garlic
⅛ teaspoon salt
⅛ teaspoon freshly ground black pepper
1 teaspoon Sriracha

1. Spray the air fryer basket lightly with olive oil. 2. In a large bowl, mix together the turkey, panko bread crumbs, egg, soy sauce, 1 tablespoon of hoisin sauce, garlic, salt, and black pepper. 3. Using a tablespoon, form 24 meatballs. 4. In a small bowl, combine the remaining 60 ml of hoisin sauce and Sriracha to make a glaze and set aside. 5. Place the meatballs in the air fryer basket in a single layer. You may need to cook them in batches. 6. Air fry at 180°C for 8 minutes. Brush the meatballs generously with the glaze and cook until cooked through, an additional 4 to 7 minutes.

Fiesta Chicken Plate

450 g boneless, skinless chicken breasts (2 large breasts)
2 tablespoons lime juice
1 teaspoon cumin
½ teaspoon salt
40 g grated Pepper Jack cheese
1 (455 g) can refried beans
130 g salsa

30 g shredded lettuce
1 medium tomato, chopped
2 avocados, peeled and sliced
1 small onion, sliced into thin rings
Sour cream
Tortilla chips (optional)

1. Split each chicken breast in half lengthwise. 2. Mix lime juice, cumin, and salt together and brush on all surfaces of chicken breasts. 3. Place in air fryer basket and air fry at 200°C for 12 to 15 minutes, until well done. 4. Divide the cheese evenly over chicken breasts and cook for an additional minute to melt cheese. 5. While chicken is cooking, heat refried beans on stovetop or in microwave. 6. When ready to serve, divide beans among 4 plates. Place chicken breasts on top of beans and spoon salsa over. Arrange the lettuce, tomatoes, and avocados artfully on each plate and scatter with the onion rings. 7. Pass sour cream at the table and serve with tortilla chips if desired.

Cheese-Encrusted Chicken Tenderloins with Peanuts

Prep time: 10 minutes | Cook time: 25 minutes | Serves 4

45 g grated Parmesan cheese
½ teaspoon garlic powder
1 teaspoon red pepper flakes
Sea salt and ground black pepper, to taste
2 tablespoons peanut oil
680 g chicken tenderloins
2 tablespoons peanuts, roasted and roughly chopped
Cooking spray

1. Preheat the air fryer to 180ºC. Spritz the air fryer basket with cooking spray. 2. Combine the Parmesan cheese, garlic powder, red pepper flakes, salt, black pepper, and peanut oil in a large bowl. Stir to mix well. 3. Dip the chicken tenderloins in the cheese mixture, then press to coat well. Shake the excess off. 4. Transfer the chicken tenderloins in the air fryer basket. Air fry for 12 minutes or until well browned. Flip the tenderloin halfway through. You may need to work in batches to avoid overcrowding. 5. Transfer the chicken tenderloins on a large plate and top with roasted peanuts before serving.

Italian Flavour Chicken Breasts with Roma Tomatoes

Prep time: 10 minutes | Cook time: 60 minutes | Serves 8

1.4 kg chicken breasts, bone-in
1 teaspoon minced fresh basil
1 teaspoon minced fresh rosemary
2 tablespoons minced fresh parsley
1 teaspoon cayenne pepper
½ teaspoon salt
½ teaspoon freshly ground black pepper
4 medium Roma tomatoes, halved
Cooking spray

1. Preheat the air fryer to 190ºC. Spritz the air fryer basket with cooking spray. 2. Combine all the ingredients, except for the chicken breasts and tomatoes, in a large bowl. Stir to mix well. 3. Dunk the chicken breasts in the mixture and press to coat well. 4. Transfer the chicken breasts in the preheated air fryer. You may need to work in batches to avoid overcrowding. 5. Air fry for 25 minutes or until the internal temperature of the thickest part of the breasts reaches at least 76ºC. Flip the breasts halfway through the cooking time. 6. Remove the cooked chicken breasts from the basket and adjust the temperature to 180ºC. 7. Place the tomatoes in the air fryer and spritz with cooking spray. Sprinkle with a touch of salt and cook for 10 minutes or until tender. Shake the basket halfway through the cooking time. 8. Serve the tomatoes with chicken breasts on a large serving plate.

Korean Honey Wings

Prep time: 10 minutes | Cook time: 25 minutes per batch | Serves 4

55 g gochujang, or red pepper paste
55 g mayonnaise
2 tablespoons honey
1 tablespoon sesame oil
2 teaspoons minced garlic
1 tablespoon sugar
2 teaspoons ground ginger
1.4 kg whole chicken wings
Olive oil spray
1 teaspoon salt
½ teaspoon freshly ground black pepper

1. In a large bowl, whisk the gochujang, mayonnaise, honey, sesame oil, garlic, sugar, and ginger. Set aside. 2. Insert the crisper plate into the basket and the basket into the unit. Preheat the unit by selecting AIR FRY, setting the temperature to 200ºC, and setting the time to 3 minutes. Select START/STOP to begin. 3. To prepare the chicken wings, cut the wings in half. The meatier part is the drumette. Cut off and discard the wing tip from the flat part (or save the wing tips in the freezer to make chicken stock). 4. Once the unit is preheated, spray the crisper plate with olive oil. Working in batches, place half the chicken wings into the basket, spray them with olive oil, and sprinkle with the salt and pepper. 5. Select AIR FRY, set the temperature to 200ºC, and set the time to 20 minutes. Select START/STOP to begin. 6. After 10 minutes, remove the basket, flip the wings, and spray them with more olive oil. Reinsert the basket to resume cooking. 7. Cook the wings to an internal temperature of 76ºC, then transfer them to the bowl with the prepared sauce and toss to coat. 8. Repeat steps 4, 5, 6, and 7 for the remaining chicken wings. 9. Return the coated wings to the basket and air fry for 4 to 6 minutes more until the sauce has glazed the wings and the chicken is crisp. After 3 minutes, check the wings to make sure they aren't burning. Serve hot.

Chicken Legs with Leeks

Prep time: 30 minutes | Cook time: 18 minutes | Serves 6

2 leeks, sliced
2 large-sized tomatoes, chopped
3 cloves garlic, minced
½ teaspoon dried oregano
6 chicken legs, boneless and
skinless
½ teaspoon smoked cayenne pepper
2 tablespoons olive oil
A freshly ground nutmeg

1. In a mixing dish, thoroughly combine all ingredients, minus the leeks. Place in the refrigerator and let it marinate overnight. 2. Lay the leeks onto the bottom of the air fryer basket. Top with the chicken legs. 3. Roast chicken legs at (190ºC for 18 minutes, turning halfway through. Serve with hoisin sauce.

Indian Fennel Chicken

Prep time: 30 minutes | Cook time: 15 minutes | Serves 4

450 g boneless, skinless chicken thighs, cut crosswise into thirds
1 yellow onion, cut into 1½-inch-thick slices
1 tablespoon coconut oil, melted
2 teaspoons minced fresh ginger
2 teaspoons minced garlic
1 teaspoon smoked paprika

1 teaspoon ground fennel
1 teaspoon garam masala
1 teaspoon ground turmeric
1 teaspoon kosher salt
½ to 1 teaspoon cayenne pepper
Vegetable oil spray
2 teaspoons fresh lemon juice
5 g chopped fresh coriander or parsley

1. Use a fork to pierce the chicken all over to allow the marinade to penetrate better. 2. In a large bowl, combine the onion, coconut oil, ginger, garlic, paprika, fennel, garam masala, turmeric, salt, and cayenne. Add the chicken, toss to combine, and marinate at room temperature for 30 minutes, or cover and refrigerate for up to 24 hours. 3. Place the chicken and onion in the air fryer basket. (Discard remaining marinade.) Spray with some vegetable oil spray. Set the air fryer to 180°C for 15 minutes. Halfway through the cooking time, remove the basket, spray the chicken and onion with more vegetable oil spray, and toss gently to coat. At the end of the cooking time, use a meat thermometer to ensure the chicken has reached an internal temperature of 76°C. 4. Transfer the chicken and onion to a serving platter. Sprinkle with the lemon juice and coriander and serve.

Porchetta-Style Chicken Breasts

Prep time: 10 minutes | Cook time: 15 minutes | Serves 4

25 g fresh parsley leaves
10 g roughly chopped fresh chives
4 cloves garlic, peeled
2 tablespoons lemon juice
3 teaspoons fine sea salt
1 teaspoon dried rubbed sage
1 teaspoon fresh rosemary leaves

1 teaspoon ground fennel
½ teaspoon red pepper flakes
4 (115 g) boneless, skinless chicken breasts, pounded to ¼ inch thick
8 slices bacon
Sprigs of fresh rosemary, for garnish (optional)

1. Spray the air fryer basket with avocado oil. Preheat the air fryer to 170°C. 2. Place the parsley, chives, garlic, lemon juice, salt, sage, rosemary, fennel, and red pepper flakes in a food processor and purée until a smooth paste forms. 3. Place the chicken breasts on a cutting board and rub the paste all over the tops. With a short end facing you, roll each breast up like a jelly roll to make a log

and secure it with toothpicks. 4. Wrap 2 slices of bacon around each chicken breast log to cover the entire breast. Secure the bacon with toothpicks. 5. Place the chicken breast logs in the air fryer basket and air fry for 5 minutes, flip the logs over, and cook for another 5 minutes. Increase the heat to 200°C and cook until the bacon is crisp, about 5 minutes more. 6. Remove the toothpicks and garnish with fresh rosemary sprigs, if desired, before serving. Store leftovers in an airtight container in the refrigerator for up to 4 days or in the freezer for up to a month. Reheat in a preheated 180°C air fryer for 5 minutes, then increase the heat to 200°C and cook for 2 minutes to crisp the bacon.

Chicken Patties

Prep time: 15 minutes | Cook time: 12 minutes | Serves 4

450 g chicken thigh mince
110 g shredded Mozzarella cheese
1 teaspoon dried parsley

½ teaspoon garlic powder
¼ teaspoon onion powder
1 large egg
60 g pork rinds, finely ground

1. In a large bowl, mix chicken mince, Mozzarella, parsley, garlic powder, and onion powder. Form into four patties. 2. Place patties in the freezer for 15 to 20 minutes until they begin to firm up. 3. Whisk egg in a medium bowl. Place the ground pork rinds into a large bowl. 4. Dip each chicken patty into the egg and then press into pork rinds to fully coat. Place patties into the air fryer basket. 5. Adjust the temperature to 180°C and air fry for 12 minutes. 6. Patties will be firm and cooked to an internal temperature of 76°C when done. Serve immediately.

Tex-Mex Chicken Breasts

Prep time: 10 minutes | Cook time: 17 to 20 minutes | Serves 4

450 g low-sodium boneless, skinless chicken breasts, cut into 1-inch cubes
1 medium onion, chopped
1 red bell pepper, chopped
1 jalapeño pepper, minced

2 teaspoons olive oil
115 g canned low-sodium black beans, rinsed and drained
130 g low-sodium salsa
2 teaspoons chili powder

1. Preheat the air fryer to 200°C. 2. In a medium metal bowl, mix the chicken, onion, bell pepper, jalapeño, and olive oil. Roast for 10 minutes, stirring once during cooking. 3. Add the black beans, salsa, and chili powder. Roast for 7 to 10 minutes more, stirring once, until the chicken reaches an internal temperature of 76°C on a meat thermometer. Serve immediately.

Chicken with Pineapple and Peach

Prep time: 10 minutes | Cook time: 14 to 15 minutes | Serves 4

1 (450 g) low-sodium boneless, skinless chicken breasts, cut into 1-inch pieces	safflower oil
	1 peach, peeled, pitted, and cubed
1 medium red onion, chopped	1 tablespoon cornflour
1 (230 g) can pineapple chunks, drained, 60 ml juice reserved	½ teaspoon ground ginger
	¼ teaspoon ground allspice
1 tablespoon peanut oil or	Brown rice, cooked (optional)

1. Preheat the air fryer to 196ºC. 2. In a medium metal bowl, mix the chicken, red onion, pineapple, and peanut oil. Bake in the air fryer for 9 minutes. Remove and stir. 3. Add the peach and return the bowl to the air fryer. Bake for 3 minutes more. Remove and stir again. 4. In a small bowl, whisk the reserved pineapple juice, the cornflour, ginger, and allspice well. Add to the chicken mixture and stir to combine. 5. Bake for 2 to 3 minutes more, or until the chicken reaches an internal temperature of 76ºC on a meat thermometer and the sauce is slightly thickened. 6. Serve immediately over hot cooked brown rice, if desired.

Brazilian Tempero Baiano Chicken Drumsticks

Prep time: 30 minutes | Cook time: 20 minutes | Serves 4

1 teaspoon cumin seeds	½ teaspoon black peppercorns
1 teaspoon dried oregano	½ teaspoon cayenne pepper
1 teaspoon dried parsley	60 ml fresh lime juice
1 teaspoon ground turmeric	2 tablespoons olive oil
½ teaspoon coriander seeds	680 g chicken drumsticks
1 teaspoon kosher salt	

1. In a clean coffee grinder or spice mill, combine the cumin, oregano, parsley, turmeric, coriander seeds, salt, peppercorns, and cayenne. Process until finely ground. 2. In a small bowl, combine the ground spices with the lime juice and oil. Place the chicken in a resealable plastic bag. Add the marinade, seal, and massage until the chicken is well coated. Marinate at room temperature for 30 minutes or in the refrigerator for up to 24 hours. 3. When you are ready to cook, place the drumsticks skin side up in the air fryer basket. Set the air fryer to 200ºC for 20 to 25 minutes, turning the legs halfway through the cooking time. Use a meat thermometer to ensure that the chicken has reached an internal temperature of 76ºC. 4. Serve with plenty of napkins.

Chicken and Vegetable Fajitas

Prep time: 15 minutes | Cook time: 23 minutes | Serves 6

Chicken:	1 tablespoon vegetable oil
450 g boneless, skinless chicken thighs, cut crosswise into thirds	½ teaspoon kosher salt
	½ teaspoon ground cumin
1 tablespoon vegetable oil	For Serving:
4½ teaspoons taco seasoning	Tortillas
Vegetables:	Sour cream
50 g sliced onion	Shredded cheese
150 g sliced bell pepper	Guacamole
1 or 2 jalapeños, quartered lengthwise	Salsa

1. For the chicken: In a medium bowl, toss together the chicken, vegetable oil, and taco seasoning to coat. 2. For the vegetables: In a separate bowl, toss together the onion, bell pepper, jalapeño(s), vegetable oil, salt, and cumin to coat. 3. Place the chicken in the air fryer basket. Set the air fryer to (190ºC for 10 minutes. Add the vegetables to the basket, toss everything together to blend the seasonings, and set the air fryer for 13 minutes more. Use a meat thermometer to ensure the chicken has reached an internal temperature of 76ºC. 4. Transfer the chicken and vegetables to a serving platter. Serve with tortillas and the desired fajita fixings.

Lemon Chicken with Garlic

Prep time: 5 minutes | Cook time: 20 to 25 minutes | Serves 4

8 bone-in chicken thighs, skin on	½ teaspoon paprika
	½ teaspoon garlic powder
1 tablespoon olive oil	¼ teaspoon freshly ground black pepper
1½ teaspoons lemon-pepper seasoning	Juice of ½ lemon

1. Preheat the air fryer to 180ºC. 2. Place the chicken in a large bowl and drizzle with the olive oil. Top with the lemon-pepper seasoning, paprika, garlic powder, and freshly ground black pepper. Toss until thoroughly coated. 3. Working in batches if necessary, arrange the chicken in a single layer in the basket of the air fryer. Pausing halfway through the cooking time to turn the chicken, air fry for 20 to 25 minutes, until a thermometer inserted into the thickest piece registers 76ºC. 4. Transfer the chicken to a serving platter and squeeze the lemon juice over the top.

Chicken, Courgette, and Spinach Salad

Prep time: 10 minutes | Cook time: 20 minutes | Serves 4

3 (140 g) boneless, skinless chicken breasts, cut into 1-inch cubes

5 teaspoons extra-virgin olive oil

½ teaspoon dried thyme

1 medium red onion, sliced

1 red bell pepper, sliced

1 small courgette, cut into strips

3 tablespoons freshly squeezed lemon juice

85 g fresh baby spinach leaves

1. Insert the crisper plate into the basket and the basket into the unit. Preheat the unit by selecting AIR ROAST, setting the temperature to 190°C, and setting the time to 3 minutes. Select START/STOP to begin. 2. In a large bowl, combine the chicken, olive oil, and thyme. Toss to coat. Transfer to a medium metal bowl that fits into the basket. 3. Once the unit is preheated, place the bowl into the basket. 4. Select AIR ROAST, set the temperature to 190°C, and set the time to 20 minutes. Select START/STOP to begin. 5. After 8 minutes, add the red onion, red bell pepper, and courgette to the bowl. Resume cooking. After about 6 minutes more, stir the chicken and vegetables. Resume cooking. 6. When the cooking is complete, a food thermometer inserted into the chicken should register at least 76°C. Remove the bowl from the unit and stir in the lemon juice. 7. Put the spinach in a serving bowl and top with the chicken mixture. Toss to combine and serve immediately.

Buttermilk-Fried Drumsticks

Prep time: 10 minutes | Cook time: 25 minutes | Serves 2

1 egg

120 g buttermilk

45 g self-rising flour

45 g seasoned panko bread crumbs

1 teaspoon salt

¼ teaspoon ground black pepper (to mix into coating)

4 chicken drumsticks, skin on

Oil for misting or cooking spray

1. Beat together egg and buttermilk in shallow dish. 2. In a second shallow dish, combine the flour, panko crumbs, salt, and pepper. 3. Sprinkle chicken legs with additional salt and pepper to taste. 4. Dip legs in buttermilk mixture, then roll in panko mixture, pressing in crumbs to make coating stick. Mist with oil or cooking spray. 5. Spray the air fryer basket with cooking spray. 6. Cook drumsticks at 180°C for 10 minutes. Turn pieces over and cook an additional 10 minutes. 7. Turn pieces to check for browning. If you have any white spots that haven't begun to brown, spritz them with oil or cooking spray. Continue cooking for 5 more minutes or until crust is golden brown and juices run clear. Larger, meatier drumsticks will take longer to cook than small ones.

Chapter 3 Beef, Pork, and Lamb

Chapter 3 Beef, Pork, and Lamb

Crescent Dogs

Prep time: 15 minutes | Cook time: 8 minutes |
Makes 24 crescent dogs

Oil, for spraying
1 (230 g) can ready-to-bake croissants
8 slices Cheddar cheese, cut into thirds

24 cocktail sausages or 8 (6-inch) hot dogs, cut into thirds
2 tablespoons unsalted melted butter
1 tablespoon sea salt flakes

1. Line the air fryer basket with parchment and spray lightly with oil. 2. Separate the dough into 8 triangles. Cut each triangle into 3 narrow triangles so you have 24 total triangles. 3. Top each triangle with 1 piece of cheese and 1 cocktail sausage. 4. Roll up each piece of dough, starting at the wide end and rolling toward the point. 5. Place the rolls in the prepared basket in a single layer. You may need to cook in batches, depending on the size of your air fryer. 6. Air fry at 160ºC for 3 to 4 minutes, flip, and cook for another 3 to 4 minutes, or until golden brown. 7. Brush with the melted butter and sprinkle with the sea salt flakes before serving.

Beef Mince Taco Rolls

Prep time: 20 minutes | Cook time: 10 minutes |
Serves 4

230 g 80/20 beef mince
80 ml water
1 tablespoon chili powder
2 teaspoons cumin
½ teaspoon garlic powder
¼ teaspoon dried oregano
60 g tinned diced tomatoes
2 tablespoons chopped

coriander
355 g shredded Mozzarella cheese
60 g blanched finely ground almond flour
60 g full-fat cream cheese
1 large egg

1. In a medium skillet over medium heat, brown the beef mince about 7 to 10 minutes. When meat is fully cooked, drain. 2. Add water to skillet and stir in chili powder, cumin, garlic powder, oregano, and tomatoes. Add coriander. Bring to a boil, then reduce heat to simmer for 3 minutes. 3. In a large microwave-safe bowl, place Mozzarella, almond flour, cream cheese, and egg. Microwave

for 1 minute. Stir the mixture quickly until smooth ball of dough forms. 4. Cut a piece of parchment for your work surface. Press the dough into a large rectangle on the parchment, wetting your hands to prevent the dough from sticking as necessary. Cut the dough into eight rectangles. 5. On each rectangle place a few spoons of the meat mixture. Fold the short ends of each roll toward the center and roll the length as you would a burrito. 6. Cut a piece of parchment to fit your air fryer basket. Place taco rolls onto the parchment and place into the air fryer basket. 7. Adjust the temperature to 180ºC and air fry for 10 minutes. 8. Flip halfway through the cooking time. 9. Allow to cool 10 minutes before serving.

Sesame Beef Lettuce Tacos

Prep time: 30 minutes | Cook time: 8 to 10 minutes |
Serves 4

60 ml soy sauce or tamari
60 ml avocado oil
2 tablespoons cooking sherry
1 tablespoon granulated sweetener
1 tablespoon ground cumin
1 teaspoon minced garlic
Sea salt and freshly ground black pepper, to taste

450 g bavette or skirt steak
8 butterhead lettuce leaves
2 spring onions, sliced
1 tablespoon toasted sesame seeds
Hot sauce, for serving
Lime wedges, for serving
Flaky sea salt (optional)

1. In a small bowl, whisk together the soy sauce, avocado oil, cooking sherry, sweetener, cumin, garlic, and salt and pepper to taste. 2. Place the steak in a shallow dish. Pour the marinade over the beef. Cover the dish with plastic wrap and let it marinate in the refrigerator for at least 2 hours or overnight. 3. Remove the flank steak from the dish and discard the marinade. 4. Set the air fryer to 200ºC. Place the steak in the air fryer basket and air fry for 4 to 6 minutes. Flip the steak and cook for 4 minutes more, until an instant-read thermometer reads 49ºC at the thickest part (or cook it to your desired doneness). Allow the steak to rest for 10 minutes, then slice it thinly against the grain. 5. Stack 2 lettuce leaves on top of each other and add some sliced meat. Top with spring onions and sesame seeds. Drizzle with hot sauce and lime juice, and finish with a little flaky salt (if using). Repeat with the remaining lettuce leaves and fillings.

BBQ Pork Steaks

Prep time: 5 minutes | Cook time: 15 minutes | Serves 4

4 pork steaks
1 tablespoon Cajun seasoning
2 tablespoons BBQ sauce
1 tablespoon vinegar
1 teaspoon soy sauce
96 g brown sugar
120 ml ketchup

1. Preheat the air fryer to 140°C. 2. Sprinkle pork steaks with Cajun seasoning. 3. Combine remaining ingredients and brush onto steaks. 4. Add coated steaks to air fryer. Air fry 15 minutes until just browned. 5. Serve immediately.

Onion Pork Kebabs

Prep time: 22 minutes | Cook time: 18 minutes | Serves 3

2 tablespoons tomato purée
½ fresh green chilli, minced
⅓ teaspoon paprika
450 g pork mince
120 g spring onions, finely chopped
3 cloves garlic, peeled and finely minced
1 teaspoon ground black pepper, or more to taste
1 teaspoon salt, or more to taste

1. Thoroughly combine all ingredients in a mixing dish. Then form your mixture into sausage shapes. 2. Cook for 18 minutes at 180°C. Mound salad on a serving platter, top with air-fried kebabs and serve warm. Bon appétit!

Almond and Caraway Crust Steak

Prep time: 16 minutes | Cook time: 10 minutes | Serves 4

40 g almond flour
2 eggs
2 teaspoons caraway seeds
4 beef steaks
2 teaspoons garlic powder
1 tablespoon melted butter
Fine sea salt and cayenne pepper, to taste

1. Generously coat steaks with garlic powder, caraway seeds, salt, and cayenne pepper. 2. In a mixing dish, thoroughly combine melted butter with seasoned crumbs. In another bowl, beat the eggs until they're well whisked. 3. First, coat steaks with the beaten egg; then, coat beef steaks with the buttered crumb mixture. Place the steaks in the air fryer basket; cook for 10 minutes at 180°C. Bon appétit!

Steak with Bell Pepper

Prep time: 30 minutes | Cook time: 20 to 23 minutes | Serves 6

60 ml avocado oil
60 g freshly squeezed lime juice
2 teaspoons minced garlic
1 tablespoon chili powder
½ teaspoon ground cumin
Sea salt and freshly ground black pepper, to taste
450 g top rump steak or bavette
or skirt steak, thinly sliced against the grain
1 red pepper, cored, seeded, and cut into ½-inch slices
1 green pepper, cored, seeded, and cut into ½-inch slices
1 large onion, sliced

1. In a small bowl or blender, combine the avocado oil, lime juice, garlic, chili powder, cumin, and salt and pepper to taste. 2. Place the sliced steak in a zip-top bag or shallow dish. Place the peppers and onion in a separate zip-top bag or dish. Pour half the marinade over the steak and the other half over the vegetables. Seal both bags and let the steak and vegetables marinate in the refrigerator for at least 1 hour or up to 4 hours. 3. Line the air fryer basket with an air fryer liner or aluminum foil. Remove the vegetables from their bag or dish and shake off any excess marinade. Set the air fryer to 200°C. Place the vegetables in the air fryer basket and cook for 13 minutes. 4. Remove the steak from its bag or dish and shake off any excess marinade. Place the steak on top of the vegetables in the air fryer, and cook for 7 to 10 minutes or until an instant-read thermometer reads 49°C for medium-rare (or cook to your desired doneness). 5. Serve with desired fixings, such as keto tortillas, lettuce, sour cream, avocado slices, shredded Cheddar cheese, and coriander.

Italian Lamb Chops with Avocado Mayo

Prep time: 5 minutes | Cook time: 12 minutes | Serves 2

2 lamp chops
2 teaspoons Italian herbs
2 avocados
120 ml mayonnaise
1 tablespoon lemon juice

1. Season the lamb chops with the Italian herbs, then set aside for 5 minutes. 2. Preheat the air fryer to 200°C and place the rack inside. 3. Put the chops on the rack and air fry for 12 minutes. 4. In the meantime, halve the avocados and open to remove the pits. Spoon the flesh into a blender. 5. Add the mayonnaise and lemon juice and pulse until a smooth consistency is achieved. 6. Take care when removing the chops from the air fryer, then plate up and serve with the avocado mayo.

Mozzarella Stuffed Beef and Pork Meatballs

Prep time: 15 minutes | Cook time: 12 minutes | Serves 4 to 6

1 tablespoon olive oil	½ teaspoon dried oregano
1 small onion, finely chopped	1½ teaspoons salt
1 to 2 cloves garlic, minced	Freshly ground black pepper, to taste
340 g beef mince	2 eggs, lightly beaten
340 g pork mince	140 g low-moisture Mozzarella or other melting cheese, cut into 1-inch cubes
90 g bread crumbs	
60 g grated Parmesan cheese	
60 g finely chopped fresh parsley	

1. Preheat a skillet over medium-high heat. Add the oil and cook the onion and garlic until tender, but not browned. 2. Transfer the onion and garlic to a large bowl and add the beef, pork, bread crumbs, Parmesan cheese, parsley, oregano, salt, pepper and eggs. Mix well until all the ingredients are combined. Divide the mixture into 12 evenly sized balls. Make one meatball at a time, by pressing a hole in the meatball mixture with the finger and pushing a piece of Mozzarella cheese into the hole. Mold the meat back into a ball, enclosing the cheese. 3. Preheat the air fryer to 190°C. 4. Working in two batches, transfer six of the meatballs to the air fryer basket and air fry for 12 minutes, shaking the basket and turning the meatballs twice during the cooking process. Repeat with the remaining 6 meatballs. Serve warm.

Italian Sausages with Peppers and Onions

Prep time: 5 minutes | Cook time: 28 minutes | Serves 3

1 medium onion, thinly sliced	coconut oil
1 yellow or orange pepper, thinly sliced	1 teaspoon fine sea salt
1 red pepper, thinly sliced	6 Italian-seasoned sausages
60 ml avocado oil or melted	Dijon mustard, for serving (optional)

1. Preheat the air fryer to 200°C. 2. Place the onion and peppers in a large bowl. Drizzle with the oil and toss well to coat the veggies. Season with the salt. 3. Place the onion and peppers in a pie pan and cook in the air fryer for 8 minutes, stirring halfway through. Remove from the air fryer and set aside. 4. Spray the air fryer basket with avocado oil. Place the sausages in the air fryer basket and air fry for 20 minutes, or until crispy and golden brown. During the last minute or two of cooking, add the onion and peppers to the basket with the sausages to warm them through. 5. Place the onion and peppers on a serving platter and arrange the sausages on top. Serve Dijon mustard on the side, if desired. 6. Store leftovers in an airtight container in the fridge for up to 7 days or in the freezer for up to a month. Reheat in a preheated 200°C air fryer for 3 minutes, or until heated through.

Fillet with Crispy Shallots

Prep time: 30 minutes | Cook time: 18 to 20 minutes | Serves 6

680 g beef fillet steaks	4 medium shallots
Sea salt and freshly ground black pepper, to taste	1 teaspoon olive oil or avocado oil

1. Season both sides of the steaks with salt and pepper, and let them sit at room temperature for 45 minutes. 2. Set the air fryer to 200°C and let it preheat for 5 minutes. 3. Working in batches if necessary, place the steaks in the air fryer basket in a single layer and air fry for 5 minutes. Flip and cook for 5 minutes longer, until an instant-read thermometer inserted in the center of the steaks registers 49°C for medium-rare (or as desired). Remove the steaks and tent with aluminum foil to rest. 4. Set the air fryer to 150°C. In a medium bowl, toss the shallots with the oil. Place the shallots in the basket and air fry for 5 minutes, then give them a toss and cook for 3 to 5 minutes more, until crispy and golden brown. 5. Place the steaks on serving plates and arrange the shallots on top.

Chuck Kebab with Rocket

Prep time: 30 minutes | Cook time: 25 minutes | Serves 4

120 g leeks, chopped	½ teaspoon ground sumac
2 garlic cloves, smashed	3 saffron threads
900 g beef mince	2 tablespoons loosely packed fresh flat-leaf parsley leaves
Salt, to taste	4 tablespoons tahini sauce
¼ teaspoon ground black pepper, or more to taste	110 g baby rocket
1 teaspoon cayenne pepper	1 tomato, cut into slices

1. In a bowl, mix the chopped leeks, garlic, beef mince, and spices; knead with your hands until everything is well incorporated. 2. Now, mound the beef mixture around a wooden skewer into a pointed-ended sausage. 3. Cook in the preheated air fryer at 180°C for 25 minutes. Serve your kebab with the tahini sauce, baby rocket and tomato. Enjoy!

Blackened Steak Nuggets

Prep time: 10 minutes | Cook time: 7 minutes | Serves 2

450 g rib eye steak, cut into 1-inch cubes
2 tablespoons salted melted butter
½ teaspoon paprika
½ teaspoon salt
¼ teaspoon garlic powder
¼ teaspoon onion granules
¼ teaspoon ground black pepper
⅛ teaspoon cayenne pepper

1. Place steak into a large bowl and pour in butter. Toss to coat. Sprinkle with remaining ingredients. 2. Place bites into ungreased air fryer basket. Adjust the temperature to 200ºC and air fry for 7 minutes, shaking the basket three times during cooking. Steak will be crispy on the outside and browned when done and internal temperature is at least 64ºC for medium and 82ºC for well-done. Serve warm.

Herb-Roasted Beef Tips with Onions

Prep time: 5 minutes | Cook time: 10 minutes | Serves 4

450 g rib eye steak, cubed
2 garlic cloves, minced
2 tablespoons olive oil
1 tablespoon fresh oregano
1 teaspoon salt
½ teaspoon black pepper
1 brown onion, thinly sliced

1. Preheat the air fryer to 190ºC. 2. In a medium bowl, combine the steak, garlic, olive oil, oregano, salt, pepper, and onion. Mix until all of the beef and onion are well coated. 3. Put the seasoned steak mixture into the air fryer basket. Roast for 5 minutes. Stir and roast for 5 minutes more. 4. Let rest for 5 minutes before serving with some favourite sides.

Parmesan-Crusted Pork Chops

Prep time: 5 minutes | Cook time: 12 minutes | Serves 4

1 large egg
120 g grated Parmesan cheese
4 (110 g) boneless pork chops
½ teaspoon salt
¼ teaspoon ground black pepper

1. Whisk egg in a medium bowl and place Parmesan in a separate medium bowl. 2. Sprinkle pork chops on both sides with salt and pepper. Dip each pork chop into egg, then press both sides into Parmesan. 3. Place pork chops into ungreased air fryer basket.

Adjust the temperature to 200ºC and air fry for 12 minutes, turning chops halfway through cooking. Pork chops will be golden and have an internal temperature of at least 64ºC when done. Serve warm.

Beef and Goat Cheese Stuffed Peppers

Prep time: 10 minutes | Cook time: 30 minutes | Serves 4

450 g lean beef mince
120 g cooked brown rice
2 plum tomatoes, diced
3 garlic cloves, minced
½ brown onion, diced
2 tablespoons fresh oregano, chopped
1 teaspoon salt
½ teaspoon black pepper
¼ teaspoon ground allspice
2 peppers, halved and seeded
110 g goat cheese
60 g fresh parsley, chopped

1. Preheat the air fryer to 180ºC. 2. In a large bowl, combine the beef, rice, tomatoes, garlic, onion, oregano, salt, pepper, and allspice. Mix well. 3. Divide the beef mixture equally into the halved peppers and top each with about a quarter of the goat cheese. 4. Place the peppers into the air fryer basket in a single layer, making sure that they don't touch each other. Bake for 30 minutes. 5. Remove the peppers from the air fryer and top with fresh parsley before serving.

Lemony Pork Loin Chop Schnitzel

Prep time: 15 minutes | Cook time: 15 minutes | Serves 4

4 thin boneless pork loin chops
2 tablespoons lemon juice
60 g flour
¼ teaspoon marjoram
1 teaspoon salt
120 g panko breadcrumbs
2 eggs
Lemon wedges, for serving
Cooking spray

1. Preheat the air fryer to 200ºC and spritz with cooking spray. 2. On a clean work surface, drizzle the pork chops with lemon juice on both sides. 3. Combine the flour with marjoram and salt on a shallow plate. Pour the breadcrumbs on a separate shallow dish. Beat the eggs in a large bowl. 4. Dredge the pork chops in the flour, then dunk in the beaten eggs to coat well. Shake the excess off and roll over the breadcrumbs. 5. Arrange the chops in the preheated air fryer and spritz with cooking spray. Air fry for 15 minutes or until the chops are golden and crispy. Flip the chops halfway through. Squeeze the lemon wedges over the fried chops and serve immediately.

Bacon-Wrapped Pork Tenderloin

Prep time: 30 minutes | Cook time: 22 to 25 minutes | Serves 6

120 g minced onion
120 ml apple cider, or apple juice
60 ml honey
1 tablespoon minced garlic
¼ teaspoon salt
¼ teaspoon freshly ground black pepper
900 g pork tenderloin
1 to 2 tablespoons oil
8 uncooked bacon slices

1. In a medium bowl, stir together the onion, cider, honey, garlic, salt, and pepper. Transfer to a large resealable bag or airtight container and add the pork. Seal the bag. Refrigerate to marinate for at least 2 hours. 2. Preheat the air fryer to 200ºC. Line the air fryer basket with parchment paper. 3. Remove the pork from the marinade and place it on the parchment. Spritz with oil. 4. Cook for 15 minutes. 5. Wrap the bacon slices around the pork and secure them with toothpicks. Turn the pork roast and spritz with oil. Cook for 7 to 10 minutes more until the internal temperature reaches 64ºC, depending on how well-done you like pork loin. It will continue cooking after it's removed from the fryer, so let it sit for 5 minutes before serving.

Steaks with Walnut-Blue Cheese Butter

Prep time: 30 minutes | Cook time: 10 minutes | Serves 6

120 g unsalted butter, at room temperature
120 g crumbled blue cheese
2 tablespoons finely chopped walnuts
1 tablespoon minced fresh rosemary
1 teaspoon minced garlic
¼ teaspoon cayenne pepper
Sea salt and freshly ground black pepper, to taste
680 g sirloin steaks, at room temperature

1. In a medium bowl, combine the butter, blue cheese, walnuts, rosemary, garlic, and cayenne pepper and salt and black pepper to taste. Use clean hands to ensure that everything is well combined. Place the mixture on a sheet of parchment paper and form it into a log. Wrap it tightly in plastic wrap. Refrigerate for at least 2 hours or freeze for 30 minutes. 2. Season the steaks generously with salt and pepper. 3. Place the air fryer basket or grill pan in the air fryer. Set the air fryer to 200ºC and let it preheat for 5 minutes. 4. Place the steaks in the basket in a single layer and air fry for 5 minutes. Flip the steaks, and cook for 5 minutes more, until an instant-read thermometer reads 49ºC for medium-rare (or as desired). 5. Transfer the steaks to a plate. Cut the butter into pieces and place the desired amount on top of the steaks. Tent a piece of aluminum foil over the steaks and allow to sit for 10 minutes before serving. 6. Store any remaining butter in a sealed container in the refrigerator for up to 2 weeks.

Cajun Bacon Pork Loin Fillet

Prep time: 30 minutes | Cook time: 20 minutes | Serves 6

680 g pork loin fillet or pork tenderloin
3 tablespoons olive oil
2 tablespoons Cajun spice mix
Salt, to taste
6 slices bacon
Olive oil spray

1. Cut the pork in half so that it will fit in the air fryer basket. 2. Place both pieces of meat in a resealable plastic bag. Add the oil, Cajun seasoning, and salt to taste, if using. Seal the bag and massage to coat all of the meat with the oil and seasonings. Marinate in the refrigerator for at least 1 hour or up to 24 hours. 3. Remove the pork from the bag and wrap 3 bacon slices around each piece. Spray the air fryer basket with olive oil spray. Place the meat in the air fryer. Set the air fryer to 180ºC for 15 minutes. Increase the temperature to 200ºC for 5 minutes. Use a meat thermometer to ensure the meat has reached an internal temperature of 64ºC. 4. Let the meat rest for 10 minutes. Slice into 6 medallions and serve.

Panko Crusted Calf's Liver Strips

Prep time: 15 minutes | Cook time: 23 to 25 minutes | Serves 4

450 g sliced calf's liver, cut into ½-inch wide strips
2 eggs
2 tablespoons milk
60 g whole wheat flour
240 g panko breadcrumbs
Salt and ground black pepper, to taste
Cooking spray

1. Preheat the air fryer to 200ºC and spritz with cooking spray. 2. Rub the calf's liver strips with salt and ground black pepper on a clean work surface. 3. Whisk the eggs with milk in a large bowl. Pour the flour in a shallow dish. Pour the panko on a separate shallow dish. 4. Dunk the liver strips in the flour, then in the egg mixture. Shake the excess off and roll the strips over the panko to coat well. 5. Arrange half of the liver strips in a single layer in the preheated air fryer and spritz with cooking spray. 6. Air fry for 5 minutes or until browned. Flip the strips halfway through. Repeat with the remaining strips. 7. Serve immediately.

Sausage-Stuffed Peppers

Prep time: 15 minutes | Cook time: 28 to 30 minutes | Serves 6

Avocado oil spray
230 g Italian-seasoned sausage, casings removed
120 g chopped mushrooms
60 g diced onion
1 teaspoon Italian seasoning
Sea salt and freshly ground

black pepper, to taste
235 ml keto-friendly marinara sauce
3 peppers, halved and seeded
85 g low-moisture Mozzarella or other melting cheese, shredded

1. Spray a large skillet with oil and place it over medium-high heat. Add the sausage and cook for 5 minutes, breaking up the meat with a wooden spoon. Add the mushrooms, onion, and Italian seasoning, and season with salt and pepper. Cook for 5 minutes more. Stir in the marinara sauce and cook until heated through. 2. Scoop the sausage filling into the pepper halves. 3. Set the air fryer to 180°C. Arrange the peppers in a single layer in the air fryer basket, working in batches if necessary. Air fry for 15 minutes. 4. Top the stuffed peppers with the cheese and air fry for 3 to 5 minutes more, until the cheese is melted and the peppers are tender.

Goat Cheese-Stuffed Bavette Steak

Prep time: 10 minutes | Cook time: 14 minutes | Serves 6

450 g bavette or skirt steak
1 tablespoon avocado oil
½ teaspoon sea salt
½ teaspoon garlic powder

¼ teaspoon freshly ground black pepper
60 g goat cheese, crumbled
235 g baby spinach, chopped

1. Place the steak in a large zip-top bag or between two pieces of plastic wrap. Using a meat mallet or heavy-bottomed skillet, pound the steak to an even ¼-inch thickness. 2. Brush both sides of the steak with the avocado oil. 3. Mix the salt, garlic powder, and pepper in a small dish. Sprinkle this mixture over both sides of the steak. 4. Sprinkle the goat cheese over top, and top that with the spinach. 5. Starting at one of the long sides, roll the steak up tightly. Tie the rolled steak with kitchen string at 3-inch intervals. 6. Set the air fryer to 200°C. Place the steak roll-up in the air fryer basket. Air fry for 7 minutes. Flip the steak and cook for an additional 7 minutes, until an instant-read thermometer reads 49°C for medium-rare (adjust the cooking time for your desired doneness).

Greek Lamb Rack

Prep time: 5 minutes | Cook time: 10 minutes | Serves 4

60 g freshly squeezed lemon juice
1 teaspoon oregano
2 teaspoons minced fresh rosemary
1 teaspoon minced fresh thyme

2 tablespoons minced garlic
Salt and freshly ground black pepper, to taste
2 to 4 tablespoons olive oil
1 lamb rib rack (7 to 8 ribs)

1. Preheat the air fryer to 180°C. 2. In a small mixing bowl, combine the lemon juice, oregano, rosemary, thyme, garlic, salt, pepper, and olive oil and mix well. 3. Rub the mixture over the lamb, covering all the meat. Put the rack of lamb in the air fryer. Roast for 10 minutes. Flip the rack halfway through. 4. After 10 minutes, measure the internal temperature of the rack of lamb reaches at least 64°C. 5. Serve immediately.

Cheese Pork Chops

Prep time: 15 minutes | Cook time: 9 to 14 minutes | Serves 4

2 large eggs
120 g finely grated Parmesan cheese
60 g finely ground blanched almond flour or finely crushed pork scratchings
1 teaspoon paprika

½ teaspoon dried oregano
½ teaspoon garlic powder
Salt and freshly ground black pepper, to taste
570 g (1-inch-thick) boneless pork chops
Avocado oil spray

1. Beat the eggs in a shallow bowl. In a separate bowl, combine the Parmesan cheese, almond flour, paprika, oregano, garlic powder, and salt and pepper to taste. 2. Dip the pork chops into the eggs, then coat them with the Parmesan mixture, gently pressing the coating onto the meat. Spray the breaded pork chops with oil. 3. Set the air fryer to 200°C. Place the pork chops in the air fryer basket in a single layer, working in batches if necessary. Cook for 6 minutes. Flip the chops and spray them with more oil. Cook for another 3 to 8 minutes, until an instant-read thermometer reads 64°C. 4. Allow the pork chops to rest for at least 5 minutes, then serve.

Chapter 4 Fish and Seafood

Chapter 4 Fish and Seafood

Crab-Stuffed Avocado Boats

Prep time: 5 minutes | Cook time: 7 minutes | Serves 4

2 medium avocados, halved and pitted
230 g cooked crab meat
¼ teaspoon Old Bay seasoning
2 tablespoons peeled and diced yellow onion
2 tablespoons mayonnaise

1. Scoop out avocado flesh in each avocado half, leaving ½ inch around edges to form a shell. Chop scooped-out avocado. 2. In a medium bowl, combine crab meat, Old Bay seasoning, onion, mayonnaise, and chopped avocado. Place ¼ mixture into each avocado shell. 3. Place avocado boats into ungreased air fryer basket. Adjust the temperature to 180ºC and air fry for 7 minutes. Avocado will be browned on the top and mixture will be bubbling when done. Serve warm.

Breaded Prawns Tacos

Prep time: 10 minutes | Cook time: 9 minutes | Makes 8 tacos

2 large eggs
1 teaspoon prepared yellow mustard
455 g small prawns, peeled, deveined, and tails removed
45 g finely shredded Gouda or Parmesan cheese
80 g pork scratchings ground to
dust
For Serving:
8 large round lettuce leaves
60 ml pico de gallo
20 g shredded purple cabbage
1 lemon, sliced
Guacamole (optional)

1. Preheat the air fryer to 200ºC. 2. Crack the eggs into a large bowl, add the mustard, and whisk until well combined. Add the prawns and stir well to coat. 3. In a medium-sized bowl, mix together the cheese and pork scratching dust until well combined. 4. One at a time, roll the coated prawns in the pork scratching dust mixture and use your hands to press it onto each prawns. Spray the coated prawns with avocado oil and place them in the air fryer basket, leaving space between them. 5. Air fry the prawns for 9 minutes, or until cooked through and no longer translucent, flipping after 4 minutes. 6. To serve, place a lettuce leaf on a serving plate, place several prawns on top, and top with 1½ teaspoons each of pico de gallo and purple cabbage. Squeeze some lemon juice on top

and serve with guacamole, if desired. 7. Store leftover prawns in an airtight container in the refrigerator for up to 3 days. Reheat in a preheated 200ºC air fryer for 5 minutes, or until warmed through.

Bacon-Wrapped Scallops

Prep time: 5 minutes | Cook time: 10 minutes | Serves 4

8 sea scallops, 30 g each, cleaned and patted dry
8 slices bacon
¼ teaspoon salt
¼ teaspoon ground black pepper

1. Wrap each scallop in 1 slice bacon and secure with a toothpick. Sprinkle with salt and pepper. 2. Place scallops into ungreased air fryer basket. Adjust the temperature to 180ºC and air fry for 10 minutes. Scallops will be opaque and firm, and have an internal temperature of 56ºC when done. Serve warm.

Tandoori Prawns

Prep time: 25 minutes | Cook time: 6 minutes | Serves 4

455 g jumbo raw prawns (21 to 25 count), peeled and deveined
1 tablespoon minced fresh ginger
3 cloves garlic, minced
5 g chopped fresh coriander or parsley, plus more for garnish
1 teaspoon ground turmeric
1 teaspoon garam masala
1 teaspoon smoked paprika
1 teaspoon kosher or coarse sea salt
½ to 1 teaspoon cayenne pepper
2 tablespoons olive oil (for Paleo) or melted ghee
2 teaspoons fresh lemon juice

1. In a large bowl, combine the prawns, ginger, garlic, coriander, turmeric, garam masala, paprika, salt, and cayenne. Toss well to coat. Add the oil or ghee and toss again. Marinate at room temperature for 15 minutes, or cover and refrigerate for up to 8 hours. 2. Place the prawns in a single layer in the air fryer basket. Set the air fryer to 160ºC for 6 minutes. Transfer the prawns to a serving platter. Cover and let the prawns finish cooking in the residual heat, about 5 minutes. 3. Sprinkle the prawns with the lemon juice and toss to coat. Garnish with additional cilantro and serve.

Sole and Cauliflower Fritters

Prep time: 5 minutes | Cook time: 24 minutes |

Serves 2

230 g sole fillets
230 g mashed cauliflower
75 g red onion, chopped
1 bell pepper, finely chopped
1 egg, beaten
2 garlic cloves, minced
2 tablespoons fresh parsley, chopped

1 tablespoon olive oil
1 tablespoon coconut aminos or tamari
½ teaspoon scotch bonnet pepper, minced
½ teaspoon paprika
Salt and white pepper, to taste
Cooking spray

1. Preheat the air fryer to 200ºC. Spray the air fryer basket with cooking spray. 2. Place the sole fillets in the basket and air fry for 10 minutes, flipping them halfway through. 3. When the fillets are done, transfer them to a large bowl. Mash the fillets into flakes. Add the remaining ingredients and stir to combine. 4. Make the fritters: Scoop out 2 tablespoons of the fish mixture and shape into a patty about ½ inch thick with your hands. Repeat with the remaining fish mixture. 5. Arrange the patties in the air fryer basket and bake for 14 minutes, flipping the patties halfway through, or until they are golden brown and cooked through. 6. Cool for 5 minutes and serve on a plate.

Air Fried Spring Rolls

Prep time: 10 minutes | Cook time: 17 to 22 minutes | Serves 4

2 teaspoons minced garlic
180 g finely sliced cabbage
50 g matchstick cut carrots
2 cans tiny prawns, 110 g each, drained

4 teaspoons soy sauce
Salt and freshly ground black pepper, to taste
16 square spring roll wrappers
Cooking spray

1. Preheat the air fryer to 190ºC. 2. Spray the air fryer basket lightly with cooking spray. Spray a medium sauté pan with cooking spray. 3. Add the garlic to the sauté pan and cook over medium heat until fragrant, 30 to 45 seconds. Add the cabbage and carrots and sauté until the vegetables are slightly tender, about 5 minutes. 4. Add the prawns and soy sauce and season with salt and pepper, then stir to combine. Sauté until the moisture has evaporated, 2 more minutes. Set aside to cool. 5. Place a spring roll wrapper on a work surface so it looks like a diamond. Place 1 tablespoon of the prawn mixture on the lower end of the wrapper. 6. Roll the wrapper away from you halfway, then fold in the right and left sides, like an envelope. Continue to roll to the very end, using a little water to seal the edge. Repeat with the remaining wrappers and filling. 7. Place the spring rolls in the air fryer basket in a single layer, leaving room between

each roll. Lightly spray with cooking spray. You may need to cook them in batches. 8. Air fry for 5 minutes. Turn the rolls over, lightly spray with cooking spray, and air fry until heated through and the rolls start to brown, 5 to 10 more minutes. Cool for 5 minutes before serving.

Fish Taco Bowl

Prep time: 10 minutes | Cook time: 12 minutes |

Serves 4

½ teaspoon salt
¼ teaspoon garlic powder
¼ teaspoon ground cumin
4 cod fillets, 110 g each
360 g finely shredded green

cabbage
735 g mayonnaise
¼ teaspoon ground black pepper
20 g chopped pickled jalapeños

1. Sprinkle salt, garlic powder, and cumin over cod and place into ungreased air fryer basket. Adjust the temperature to 180ºC and air fry for 12 minutes, turning fillets halfway through cooking. Cod will flake easily and have an internal temperature of at least 64ºC when done. 2. In a large bowl, toss cabbage with mayonnaise, pepper, and jalapeños until fully coated. Serve cod warm over cabbage slaw on four medium plates.

Panko Catfish Nuggets

Prep time: 10 minutes | Cook time: 7 to 8 minutes |

Serves 4

2 medium catfish fillets, cut into chunks (approximately 1 × 2 inch)
Salt and pepper, to taste
2 eggs

2 tablespoons skimmed milk
30 g cornflour
75 g panko bread crumbs
Cooking spray

1. Preheat the air fryer to 200ºC. 2. In a medium bowl, season the fish chunks with salt and pepper to taste. 3. In a small bowl, beat together the eggs with milk until well combined. 4. Place the cornflour and bread crumbs into separate shallow dishes. 5. Dredge the fish chunks one at a time in the cornflour, coating well on both sides, then dip in the egg mixture, shaking off any excess, finally press well into the bread crumbs. Spritz the fish chunks with cooking spray. 6. Arrange the fish chunks in the air fryer basket in a single layer. You may need to cook in batches depending on the size of your air fryer basket. 7. Fry the fish chunks for 7 to 8 minutes until they are no longer translucent in the center and golden brown. Shake the basket once during cooking. 8. Remove the fish chunks from the basket to a plate. Repeat with the remaining fish chunks. 9. Serve warm.

Bacon Halibut Steak

Prep time: 15 minutes | Cook time: 10 minutes | Serves 4

680 g halibut steaks (170 g each fillet)
1 teaspoon avocado oil

1 teaspoon ground black pepper
110 g bacon, sliced

1. Sprinkle the halibut steaks with avocado oil and ground black pepper. 2. Then wrap the fish in the bacon slices and put in the air fryer. 3. Cook the fish at 200°C for 5 minutes per side.

Lemony Salmon

Prep time: 30 minutes | Cook time: 10 minutes | Serves 4

680 g salmon steak
½ teaspoon grated lemon zest
Freshly cracked mixed peppercorns, to taste
80 ml lemon juice
Fresh chopped chives, for

garnish
120 ml dry white wine, or apple cider vinegar
½ teaspoon fresh coriander, chopped
Fine sea salt, to taste

1. To prepare the marinade, place all ingredients, except for salmon steak and chives, in a deep pan. Bring to a boil over medium-high flame until it has reduced by half. Allow it to cool down. 2. After that, allow salmon steak to marinate in the refrigerator approximately 40 minutes. Discard the marinade and transfer the fish steak to the preheated air fryer. 3. Air fry at 200°C for 9 to 10 minutes. To finish, brush hot fish steaks with the reserved marinade, garnish with fresh chopped chives, and serve right away!

Baked Grouper with Tomatoes and Garlic

Prep time: 5 minutes | Cook time: 12 minutes | Serves 4

4 grouper fillets
½ teaspoon salt
3 garlic cloves, minced
1 tomato, sliced

45 g sliced Kalamata olives
10 g fresh dill, roughly chopped
Juice of 1 lemon
¼ cup olive oil

1. Preheat the air fryer to 190°C. 2. Season the grouper fillets on all sides with salt, then place into the air fryer basket and top with the minced garlic, tomato slices, olives, and fresh dill. 3. Drizzle the lemon juice and olive oil over the top of the grouper, then bake for 10 to 12 minutes, or until the internal temperature reaches 64°C.

Tilapia Almondine

Prep time: 10 minutes | Cook time: 10 minutes | Serves 2

25 g almond flour or fine dried bread crumbs
2 tablespoons salted butter or ghee, melted
1 teaspoon black pepper
½ teaspoon kosher or coarse sea

salt
60 g mayonnaise
2 tilapia fillets
435 g thinly sliced almonds
Vegetable oil spray

1. In a small bowl, mix together the almond flour, butter, pepper and salt. 2. Spread the mayonnaise on both sides of each fish fillet. Dredge the fillets in the almond flour mixture. Spread the sliced almonds on one side of each fillet, pressing lightly to adhere. 3. Spray the air fryer basket with vegetable oil spray. Place the fish fillets in the basket. Set the air fryer to 160°C for 10 minutes, or until the fish flakes easily with a fork.

Classic Fish Sticks with Tartar Sauce

Prep time: 10 minutes | Cook time: 12 to 15 minutes | Serves 4

680 g cod fillets, cut into 1-inch strips
1 teaspoon salt
½ teaspoon freshly ground black pepper
2 eggs
35 g almond flour
20 g grated Parmesan cheese
Tartar Sauce:

120 ml sour cream
120 ml mayonnaise
3 tablespoons chopped dill pickle
2 tablespoons capers, drained and chopped
½ teaspoon dried dill
1 tablespoon dill pickle liquid (optional)

1. Preheat the air fryer to 200°C. 2. Season the cod with the salt and black pepper; set aside. 3. In a shallow bowl, lightly beat the eggs. In a second shallow bowl, combine the almond flour and Parmesan cheese. Stir until thoroughly combined. 4. Working with a few pieces at a time, dip the fish into the egg mixture followed by the flour mixture. Press lightly to ensure an even coating. 5. Working in batches if necessary, arrange the fish in a single layer in the air fryer basket and spray lightly with olive oil. Pausing halfway through the cooking time to turn the fish, air fry for 12 to 15 minutes, until the fish flakes easily with a fork. Let sit in the basket for a few minutes before serving with the tartar sauce. 6. To make the tartar sauce: In a small bowl, combine the sour cream, mayonnaise, pickle, capers, and dill. If you prefer a thinner sauce, stir in the pickle liquid.

Cod Tacos with Mango Salsa

Prep time: 15 minutes | Cook time: 17 minutes | Serves 4

1 mango, peeled and diced	1 egg
1 small jalapeño pepper, diced	75 g cornflour
½ red bell pepper, diced	90 g plain flour
½ red onion, minced	½ teaspoon ground cumin
Pinch chopped fresh cilantro	¼ teaspoon chilli powder
Juice of ½ lime	455 g cod, cut into 4 pieces
¼ teaspoon salt	Olive oil spray
¼ teaspoon ground black pepper	4 corn tortillas, or flour tortillas, at room temperature
120 ml Mexican beer	

1. In a small bowl, stir together the mango, jalapeño, red bell pepper, red onion, cilantro, lime juice, salt, and pepper. Set aside. 2. In a medium bowl, whisk the beer and egg. 3. In another medium bowl, stir together the cornflour, flour, cumin, and chilli powder. 4. Insert the crisper plate into the basket and the basket into the unit. Preheat the unit to 190ºC. 5. Dip the fish pieces into the egg mixture and in the flour mixture to coat completely. 6. Once the unit is preheated, place a baking paper liner into the basket. Place the fish on the liner in a single layer. 7. Cook for about 9 minutes, spray the fish with olive oil. Reinsert the basket to resume cooking. 8. When the cooking is complete, the fish should be golden and crispy. Place the pieces in the tortillas, top with the mango salsa, and serve.

Fish Tacos with Jalapeño-Lime Sauce

Prep time: 25 minutes | Cook time: 7 to 10 minutes | Serves 4

Fish Tacos:	Jalapeño-Lime Sauce:
455 g firm white fish fillets	120 ml sour cream
¼ teaspoon cumin	1 tablespoon lime juice
¼ teaspoon coriander	¼ teaspoon grated lime zest
⅛ teaspoon ground red pepper	½ teaspoon minced jalapeño
1 tablespoon lime zest	(flesh only)
¼ teaspoon smoked paprika	¼ teaspoon cumin
1 teaspoon oil	Napa Cabbage Garnish:
Cooking spray	90 g shredded Savoy cabbage
6 to 8 corn or flour tortillas (6-inch size)	40 g sliced red or green bell pepper
30 g sliced onion	

1. Slice the fish fillets into strips approximately ½-inch thick. 2. Put the strips into a sealable plastic bag along with the cumin, coriander, red pepper, lime zest, smoked paprika, and oil. Massage seasonings into the fish until evenly distributed. 3. Spray the air fryer basket with nonstick cooking spray and place seasoned fish inside. 4. Air fry at 200ºC for approximately 5 minutes. Shake basket to distribute fish. Cook an additional 2 to 5 minutes, until fish flakes easily. 5. While the fish is cooking, prepare the Jalapeño-Lime Sauce by mixing the sour cream, lime juice, lime zest, jalapeño, and cumin together to make a smooth sauce. Set aside. 6. Mix the cabbage, bell pepper, and onion together and set aside. 7. To warm refrigerated tortillas, wrap in damp paper towels and microwave for 30 to 60 seconds. 8. To serve, spoon some of fish into a warm tortilla. Add one or two tablespoons Napa Cabbage Garnish and drizzle with Jalapeño-Lime Sauce.

Miso Salmon

Prep time: 10 minutes | Cook time: 12 minutes | Serves 2

2 tablespoons brown sugar	black pepper
2 tablespoons soy sauce	2 salmon fillets, 140 g each
2 tablespoons white miso paste	Vegetable oil spray
1 teaspoon minced garlic	1 teaspoon sesame seeds
1 teaspoon minced fresh ginger	2 spring onions, thinly sliced,
½ teaspoon freshly cracked	for garnish

1. In a small bowl, whisk together the brown sugar, soy sauce, miso, garlic, ginger, and pepper to combine. 2. Place the salmon fillets on a plate. Pour half the sauce over the fillets; turn the fillets to coat the other sides with sauce. 3. Spray the air fryer basket with vegetable oil spray. Place the sauce-covered salmon in the basket. Set the air fryer to 200ºC for 12 minutes. Halfway through the cooking time, brush additional miso sauce on the salmon. 4. Sprinkle the salmon with the sesame seeds and spring onions and serve.

Honey-Glazed Salmon

Prep time: 5 minutes | Cook time: 12 minutes | Serves 4

60 ml raw honey	½ teaspoon salt
4 garlic cloves, minced	Olive oil cooking spray
1 tablespoon olive oil	4 (1½-inch-thick) salmon fillets

1. Preheat the air fryer to 190ºC. 2. In a small bowl, mix together the honey, garlic, olive oil, and salt. 3. Spray the bottom of the air fryer basket with olive oil cooking spray, and place the salmon in a single layer on the bottom of the air fryer basket. 4. Brush the top of each fillet with the honey-garlic mixture, and roast for 10 to 12 minutes, or until the internal temperature reaches 64ºC.

Baked Monkfish

2 teaspoons olive oil
100 g celery, sliced
2 bell peppers, sliced
1 teaspoon dried thyme
½ teaspoon dried marjoram
½ teaspoon dried rosemary
2 monkfish fillets
1 tablespoon coconut aminos,

or tamari
2 tablespoons lime juice
Coarse salt and ground black
pepper, to taste
1 teaspoon cayenne pepper
90 g Kalamata olives, pitted
and sliced

1. In a nonstick skillet, heat the olive oil for 1 minute. Once hot, sauté the celery and peppers until tender, about 4 minutes. Sprinkle with thyme, marjoram, and rosemary and set aside. 2. Toss the fish fillets with the coconut aminos, lime juice, salt, black pepper, and cayenne pepper. Place the fish fillets in the lightly greased air fryer basket and bake at 200ºC for 8 minutes. 3. Turn them over, add the olives, and cook an additional 4 minutes. Serve with the sautéed vegetables on the side. Bon appétit!

Fish Cakes

1 large russet potato, mashed
340 g cod or other white fish
Salt and pepper, to taste
Olive or vegetable oil for
misting or cooking spray
1 large egg

50 g potato starch
30 g panko breadcrumbs
1 tablespoon fresh chopped
chives
2 tablespoons minced onion

1. Peel potatoes, cut into cubes, and cook on stovetop till soft. 2. Salt and pepper raw fish to taste. Mist with oil or cooking spray, and air fry at 180ºC for 6 to 8 minutes, until fish flakes easily. If fish is crowded, rearrange halfway through cooking to ensure all pieces cook evenly. 3. Transfer fish to a plate and break apart to cool. 4. Beat egg in a shallow dish. 5. Place potato starch in another shallow dish, and panko crumbs in a third dish. 6. When potatoes are done, drain in colander and rinse with cold water. 7. In a large bowl, mash the potatoes and stir in the chives and onion. Add salt and pepper to taste, then stir in the fish. 8. If needed, stir in a tablespoon of the beaten egg to help bind the mixture. 9. Shape into 8 small, fat patties. Dust lightly with potato starch, dip in egg, and roll in panko crumbs. Spray both sides with oil or cooking spray. 10. Air fry for 10 to 12 minutes, until golden brown and crispy.

Prawn Caesar Salad

340 g fresh large prawns,
peeled and deveined
1 tablespoon plus 1 teaspoon
freshly squeezed lemon juice,
divided
4 tablespoons olive oil or
avocado oil, divided
2 garlic cloves, minced, divided
¼ teaspoon sea salt, plus
additional to season the
marinade

¼ teaspoon freshly ground
black pepper, plus additional to
season the marinade
735 g mayonnaise
2 tablespoons freshly grated
Parmesan cheese
1 teaspoon Dijon mustard
1 tinned anchovy, mashed
340 g romaine lettuce hearts,
torn

1. Place the prawns in a large bowl. Add 1 tablespoon of lemon juice, 1 tablespoon of olive oil, and 1 minced garlic clove. Season with salt and pepper. Toss well and refrigerate for 15 minutes. 2. While the prawns marinates, make the dressing: In a blender, combine the mayonnaise, Parmesan cheese, Dijon mustard, the remaining 1 teaspoon of lemon juice, the anchovy, the remaining minced garlic clove, ¼ teaspoon of salt, and ¼ teaspoon of pepper. Process until smooth. With the blender running, slowly stream in the remaining 3 tablespoons of oil. Transfer the mixture to a jar; seal and refrigerate until ready to serve. 3. Remove the prawns from its marinade and place it in the air fryer basket in a single layer. Set the air fryer to 200ºC and air fry for 2 minutes. Flip the prawns and cook for 2 to 4 minutes more, until the flesh turns opaque. 4. Place the romaine in a large bowl and toss with the desired amount of dressing. Top with the prawns and serve immediately.

Lemony Prawns

455 g prawns, peeled and
deveined
4 tablespoons olive oil
1½ tablespoons lemon juice
1½ tablespoons fresh parsley,
roughly chopped

2 cloves garlic, finely minced
1 teaspoon crushed red pepper
flakes, or more to taste
Garlic pepper, to taste
Sea salt flakes, to taste

1. Preheat the air fryer to 200ºC. 2. Toss all the ingredients in a large bowl until the prawns are coated on all sides. 3. Arrange the prawns in the air fryer basket and air fry for 7 to 8 minutes, or until the prawns are pink and cooked through. 4. Serve warm.

Sesame-Crusted Tuna Steak

Prep time: 5 minutes | Cook time: 8 minutes | Serves 2

2 tuna steaks, 170 g each
1 tablespoon coconut oil, melted

½ teaspoon garlic powder
2 teaspoons white sesame seeds
2 teaspoons black sesame seeds

1. Brush each tuna steak with coconut oil and sprinkle with garlic powder. 2. In a large bowl, mix sesame seeds and then press each tuna steak into them, covering the steak as completely as possible. Place tuna steaks into the air fryer basket. 3. Adjust the temperature to 200ºC and air fry for 8 minutes. 4. Flip the steaks halfway through the cooking time. Steaks will be well-done at 64ºC internal temperature. Serve warm.

Prawns Curry

Prep time: 30 minutes | Cook time: 10 minutes | Serves 4

180 ml unsweetened full-fat coconut milk
10 g finely chopped yellow onion
2 teaspoons garam masala
1 tablespoon minced fresh ginger
1 tablespoon minced garlic

1 teaspoon ground turmeric
1 teaspoon salt
¼ to ½ teaspoon cayenne pepper
455 g raw prawns (21 to 25 count), peeled and deveined
2 teaspoons chopped fresh coriander

1. In a large bowl, stir together the coconut milk, onion, garam masala, ginger, garlic, turmeric, salt and cayenne, until well blended. 2. Add the prawns and toss until coated with sauce on all sides. Marinate at room temperature for 30 minutes. 3. Transfer the prawns and marinade to a baking pan. Place the pan in the air fryer basket. Set the air fryer to 190ºC for 10 minutes, stirring halfway through the cooking time. 4. Transfer the prawns to a serving bowl or platter. Sprinkle with the cilantro and serve.

Crab and Bell Pepper Cakes

Prep time: 5 minutes | Cook time: 10 minutes | Serves 4

230 g jumbo lump crabmeat
1 tablespoon Old Bay seasoning
20 g bread crumbs
40 g diced red bell pepper
40 g diced green bell pepper

1 egg
60 g mayonnaise
Juice of ½ lemon
1 teaspoon plain flour
Cooking oil spray

1. Sort through the crabmeat, picking out any bits of shell or cartilage. 2. In a large bowl, stir together the Old Bay seasoning, bread crumbs, red and green bell peppers, egg, mayonnaise, and lemon juice. Gently stir in the crabmeat. 3. Insert the crisper plate into the basket and the basket into the unit. Preheat the unit to 190ºC. 4. Form the mixture into 4 patties. Sprinkle ¼ teaspoon of flour on top of each patty. 5. Once the unit is preheated, spray the crisper plate with cooking oil. Place the crab cakes into the basket and spray them with cooking oil. 6. Cook for 10 minutes. 7. When the cooking is complete, the crab cakes will be golden brown and firm.

Coconut Prawns

Prep time: 5 minutes | Cook time: 6 minutes | Serves 2

230 g medium prawns, peeled and deveined
2 tablespoons salted butter, melted

½ teaspoon Old Bay seasoning
25 g desiccated, unsweetened coconut

1. In a large bowl, toss the prawns in butter and Old Bay seasoning. 2. Place shredded coconut in bowl. Coat each piece of prawns in the coconut and place into the air fryer basket. 3. Adjust the temperature to 200ºC and air fry for 6 minutes. 4. Gently turn the prawns halfway through the cooking time. Serve immediately.

Chapter 5 Snacks and Appetizers

Chapter 5 Snacks and Appetizers

Sausage Balls with Cheese

Prep time: 10 minutes | Cook time: 10 to 11 minutes

| Serves 8

340 g mild sausage meat
177 g baking mix
120 g shredded mild Cheddar
cheese

85 g soft white cheese, at room
temperature
1 to 2 tablespoons olive oil

1. Preheat the air fryer to 160°C. Line the air fryer basket with baking paper paper. 2. Mix together the ground sausage, baking mix, Cheddar cheese, and soft white cheese in a large bowl and stir to incorporate. 3. Divide the sausage mixture into 16 equal portions and roll them into 1-inch balls with your hands. 4. Arrange the sausage balls on the baking paper, leaving space between each ball. You may need to work in batches to avoid overcrowding. 5. Brush the sausage balls with the olive oil. Bake for 10 to 11 minutes, shaking the basket halfway through, or until the balls are firm and lightly browned on both sides. 6. Remove from the basket to a plate and repeat with the remaining balls. 7. Serve warm.

Crispy Cajun Fresh Dill Pickle Chips

Prep time: 5 minutes | Cook time: 10 minutes |

Makes 16 slices

30 g plain flour
42 g panko breadcrumbs
1 large egg, beaten
2 teaspoons Cajun seasoning

2 large fresh dill pickled
cucumbers, sliced into 8 rounds
each
Cooking spray

1. Preheat the air fryer to 200°C. 2. Place the plain flour, panko breadcrumbs, and egg into 3 separate shallow dishes, then stir the Cajun seasoning into the flour. 3. Dredge each pickle chip in the flour mixture, then the egg, and finally the breadcrumbs. Shake off any excess, then place each coated pickle chip on a plate. 4. Spritz the air fryer basket with cooking spray, then place 8 pickle chips in the basket and air fry for 5 minutes, or until crispy and golden. Repeat this process with the remaining pickle chips. 5. Remove the chips and allow to slightly cool on a a wire rack before serving.

Tortellini with Spicy Dipping Sauce

Prep time: 5 minutes | Cook time: 20 minutes |

Serves 4

177 ml mayonnaise
2 tablespoons mustard
1 egg
60 g flour

½ teaspoon dried oregano
120 g breadcrumbs
2 tablespoons olive oil
475 g frozen cheese tortellini

1. Preheat the air fryer to 190°C. 2. In a small bowl, combine the mayonnaise and mustard and mix well. Set aside. 3. In a shallow dish, beat the egg. In a separate bowl, combine the flour and oregano. In another bowl, combine the breadcrumbs and olive oil, and mix well. 4. Drop the tortellini, a few at a time, into the egg, then into the flour, then into the egg again, and then into the breadcrumbs to coat. Put into the air fryer basket, cooking in batches. 5. Air fry for about 10 minutes, shaking halfway through the cooking time, or until the tortellini are crisp and golden on the outside. Serve with the mayonnaise mixture.

Cheesy Steak Fries

Prep time: 5 minutes | Cook time: 20 minutes |

Serves 5

1 (794 g) bag frozen steak fries
Cooking spray
Salt and pepper, to taste
120 ml beef gravy

90 g shredded mozzarella
cheese cheese
2 spring onions, green parts
only, chopped

1. Preheat the air fryer to 200°C. 2. Place the frozen steak fries in the air fryer. Air fry for 10 minutes. Shake the basket and spritz the fries with cooking spray. Sprinkle with salt and pepper. Air fry for an additional 8 minutes. 3. Pour the beef gravy into a medium, microwave-safe bowl. Microwave for 30 seconds, or until the gravy is warm. 4. Sprinkle the fries with the cheese. Air fry for an additional 2 minutes, until the cheese is melted. 5. Transfer the fries to a serving dish. Drizzle the fries with gravy and sprinkle the spring onions on top for a green garnish. Serve.

Crispy Mozzarella Cheese Sticks

Prep time: 8 minutes | Cook time: 5 minutes | Serves 4

65 g plain flour
1 egg, beaten
25 g panko breadcrumbs
30 g grated Parmesan cheese
1 teaspoon Italian seasoning

½ teaspoon garlic salt
6 mozzarella cheese sticks, halved crosswise
Olive oil spray

1. Put the flour in a small bowl. 2. Put the beaten egg in another small bowl. 3. In a medium-sized bowl, stir together the panko, Parmesan cheese, Italian seasoning, and garlic salt. 4. Roll a mozzarella cheese-stick half in the flour, dip it into the egg, and then roll it in the panko mixture to coat. Press the coating lightly to make sure the breadcrumbs stick to the cheese. Repeat with the remaining 11 mozzarella cheese sticks. 5. Insert the crisper plate into the basket and the basket into the unit. Preheat the unit by selecting AIR FRY, setting the temperature to 200°C, and setting the time to 3 minutes. Select START/STOP to begin. 6. Once the unit is preheated, spray the crisper plate with olive oil and place a baking paper paper liner in the basket. Place the mozzarella cheese sticks into the basket and lightly spray them with olive oil. 7. Select AIR FRY, set the temperature to 200°C, and set the time to 5 minutes. Select START/STOP to begin. 8. When the cooking is complete, the mozzarella cheese sticks should be golden and crispy. Let the sticks stand for 1 minute before transferring them to a serving plate. Serve warm.

Peppery Chicken Meatballs

Prep time: 5 minutes | Cook time: 13 to 20 minutes | Makes 16 meatballs

2 teaspoons olive oil
35 g minced onion
35 g minced red pepper
2 vanilla wafers, crushed

1 egg white
½ teaspoon dried thyme
230 g minced chicken breast

1. Preheat the air fryer to 188°C. 2. In a baking pan, mix the olive oil, onion, and red pepper. Put the pan in the air fryer. Air fry for 3 to 5 minutes, or until the mixed vegetables are tender. 3. In a medium-sized bowl, mix the cooked mixed vegetables, crushed wafers, egg white, and thyme until well combined 4. Mix in the chicken, gently but thoroughly, until everything is combined. 5. Form the mixture into 16 meatballs and place them in the air fryer basket. Air fry for 10 to 15 minutes, or until the meatballs reach an internal temperature of 70°C on a meat thermometer. 6. Serve immediately.

Golden Onion Rings

Prep time: 15 minutes | Cook time: 14 minutes per batch | Serves 4

1 large white onion, peeled and cut into ½ to ¾-inch-thick slices (about 475 g)
120 ml semi-skimmed milk
115 g wholemeal pastry flour, or plain flour
2 tablespoons cornflour
¾ teaspoon sea salt, divided
½ teaspoon freshly ground

black pepper, divided
¾ teaspoon garlic powder, divided
110 g wholemeal breadcrumbs, or gluten-free breadcrumbs
Cooking oil spray (coconut, sunflower, or safflower)
tomato ketchup, for serving (optional)

1. Carefully separate the onion slices into rings—a gentle touch is important here. 2. Place the milk in a shallow dish and set aside. 3. Make the first breading: In a medium-sized bowl, stir together the flour, cornflour, ¼ teaspoon of salt, ¼ teaspoon of pepper, and ¼ teaspoon of garlic powder. Set aside. 4. Make the second breading: In a separate medium bowl, stir together the breadcrumbs with the remaining ½ teaspoon of salt, the remaining ½ teaspoon of garlic, and the remaining ½ teaspoon of pepper. Set aside. 5. Insert the crisper plate into the basket and the basket into the unit. Preheat the unit by selecting AIR FRY, setting the temperature to 200°C, and setting the time to 3 minutes. Select START/STOP to begin. 6. Once the unit is preheated, spray the crisper plate and the basket with cooking oil. 7. To make the onion rings, dip one ring into the milk and into the first breading mixture. Dip the ring into the milk again and back into the first breading mixture, coating thoroughly. Dip the ring into the milk one last time and then into the second breading mixture, coating thoroughly. Gently lay the onion ring in the basket. Repeat with additional rings and, as you place them into the basket, do not overlap them too much. Once all the onion rings are in the basket, generously spray the tops with cooking oil. 8. Select AIR FRY, set the temperature to 200°C, and set the time to 14 minutes. Insert the basket into the unit. Select START/STOP to begin. 9. After 4 minutes, open the unit and spray the rings generously with cooking oil. Close the unit to resume cooking. After 3 minutes, remove the basket and spray the onion rings again. Remove the rings, turn them over, and place them back into the basket. Generously spray them again with oil. Reinsert the basket to resume cooking. After 4 minutes, generously spray the rings with oil one last time. Resume cooking for the remaining 3 minutes, or until the onion rings are very crunchy and brown. 10. When the cooking is complete, serve the hot rings with tomato ketchup, or other sauce of choice.

Sweet Potato Fries with Mayonnaise

Prep time: 5 minutes | Cook time: 20 minutes |
Serves 2 to 3

1 large sweet potato (about 450 g), scrubbed
1 teaspoon mixed vegetables or rapeseed oil
Salt, to taste
Dipping Sauce:

60 ml light mayonnaise
½ teaspoon sriracha sauce
1 tablespoon spicy brown mustard
1 tablespoon sweet Thai chilli sauce

1. Preheat the air fryer to 90ºC. 2. On a flat work surface, cut the sweet potato into fry-shaped strips about ¼ inch wide and ¼ inch thick. You can use a mandoline to slice the sweet potato quickly and uniformly. 3. In a medium-sized bowl, drizzle the sweet potato strips with the oil and toss well. 4. Transfer to the air fryer basket and air fry for 10 minutes, shaking the basket twice during cooking. 5. Remove the air fryer basket and sprinkle with the salt and toss to coat. 6. Increase the air fryer temperature to 200ºC and air fry for an additional 10 minutes, or until the fries are crispy and tender. Shake the basket a few times during cooking. 7. Meanwhile, whisk together all the ingredients for the sauce in a small bowl. 8. Remove the sweet potato fries from the basket to a plate and serve warm alongside the dipping sauce.

Caramelized Onion Dip with White Cheese

Prep time: 5 minutes | Cook time: 30 minutes |
Serves 8 to 10

1 tablespoon butter
one medium-sized onion, halved and thinly sliced
¼ teaspoon rock salt, plus additional for seasoning
113 g soft white cheese
120 ml soured cream

¼ teaspoon onion powder
1 tablespoon finely chopped fresh chives
Black pepper, to taste
Thickly sliced potato crisps or mixed vegetables crisps

1. Place the butter in a baking pan. Place the pan in the air fryer basket. Set the air fryer to 90ºC for 1 minute, or until the butter is melted. Add the onions and salt to the pan. 2. Set the air fryer to 90ºC for 15 minutes, or until onions are softened. Set the air fryer to 190ºC for 15 minutes, until onions are a deep golden, stirring two or three times during the cooking time. Let cool completely. 3. In a medium-sized bowl, stir together the cooked onions, soft white cheese, soured cream, onion powder, and chives. Season with salt and pepper. Cover and refrigerate for 2 hours to allow the flavours to blend. 4. Serve the dip with potato crisps or mixed vegetables crisps.

String Bean Fries

Prep time: 15 minutes | Cook time: 5 to 6 minutes |
Serves 4

227 g fresh French beans
2 eggs
4 teaspoons water
60 g plain flour
50 g breadcrumbs
¼ teaspoon salt

¼ teaspoon ground black pepper
¼ teaspoon mustard powder (optional)
Oil for misting or cooking spray

1. Preheat the air fryer to 180ºC. 2. Trim stem ends from French beans, wash, and pat dry. 3. In a shallow dish, beat eggs and water together until well blended. 4. Place flour in a second shallow dish. 5. In a third shallow dish, stir together the breadcrumbs, salt, pepper, and mustard powder if using. 6. Dip each bean in egg mixture, flour, egg mixture again, then breadcrumbs. 7. When you finish coating all the French beans, open air fryer and place them in basket. 8. Cook for 3 minutes. 9. Stop and mist French beans with oil or cooking spray. 10. Cook for 2 to 3 more minutes or until French beans are crispy and nicely browned.

Lebanese Muhammara

Prep time: 15 minutes | Cook time: 15 minutes |
Serves 6

2 large red peppers
60 ml plus 2 tablespoons extra-virgin olive oil
85 g walnut halves
1 tablespoon agave syrup or honey
1 teaspoon fresh lemon juice
1 teaspoon cumin powder

1 teaspoon rock salt
1 teaspoon red pepper flakes
Raw mixed vegetables (such as cucumber, carrots, sliced courgette, or cauliflower) or toasted pitta bread chips, for serving

1. Drizzle the peppers with 2 tablespoons of the olive oil and place in the air fryer basket. Set the air fryer to 200ºC for 10 minutes. 2. Add the walnuts to the basket, arranging them around the peppers. Set the air fryer to 200ºC for 5 minutes. 3. Remove the peppers, seal in a a resealable plastic bag, and let rest for 5 to 10 minutes. Transfer the walnuts to a plate and set aside to cool down. 4. Place the softened peppers, walnuts, agave, lemon juice, cumin, salt, and ½ teaspoon of the pepper flakes blend in a food processor until smooth. 5. Transfer the dip to a serving bowl and create an indentation in the middle. Pour the remaining 60 ml olive oil into the indentation. Garnish the dip with the remaining ½ teaspoon pepper flakes. 6. Serve with mixed vegetables or toasted pitta bread chips.

Spinach and Crab Meat Cups

Prep time: 10 minutes | Cook time: 10 minutes | Makes 30 cups

1 (170 g) can crab meat, drained to yield 80 g meat
30 g frozen spinach, thawed, drained, and chopped
1 clove garlic, minced
84 g grated Parmesan cheese
3 tablespoons plain yoghurt
¼ teaspoon lemon juice
½ teaspoon Worcestershire sauce
30 mini frozen filo shells, thawed
Cooking spray

1. Preheat the air fryer to 200ºC. 2. Remove any bits of shell that might remain in the crab meat. 3. Mix the crab meat, spinach, garlic, and cheese together. 4. Stir in the yoghurt, lemon juice, and Worcestershire sauce and mix well. 5. Spoon a teaspoon of filling into each filo shell. 6. Spray the air fryer basket with cooking spray and arrange half the shells in the basket. Air fry for 5 minutes. Repeat with the remaining shells. 7. Serve immediately.

Prawns Egg Rolls

Prep time: 15 minutes | Cook time: 10 minutes per batch | Serves 4

1 tablespoon mixed vegetables oil
½ head green or savoy cabbage, finely shredded
90 g grated carrots
240 ml canned bean sprouts, drained
1 tablespoon soy sauce
½ teaspoon sugar
1 teaspoon sesame oil
60 ml hoisin sauce
Freshly ground black pepper, to taste
454 g cooked prawns, diced
30 g spring onions
8 egg roll wrappers (or use spring roll pastry)
mixed vegetables oil
Duck sauce

1. Preheat a large sauté pan over medium-high heat. Add the oil and cook the cabbage, carrots and bean sprouts until they start to wilt, about 3 minutes. Add the soy sauce, sugar, sesame oil, hoisin sauce and black pepper. Sauté for a few more minutes. Stir in the prawns and spring onions and cook until the mixed vegetables are just tender. Transfer the mixture to a colander in a bowl to cool. Press or squeeze out any excess water from the filling so that you don't end up with soggy egg rolls. 2. Make the egg rolls: Place the egg roll wrappers on a flat surface with one of the points facing towards you so they look like diamonds. Dividing the filling evenly between the eight wrappers, spoon the mixture onto the centre of the egg roll wrappers. Spread the filling across the centre of the wrappers from the left corner to the right corner but leave 2 inches from each corner empty. Brush the empty sides of the wrapper with a little

water. Fold the bottom corner of the wrapper tightly up over the filling, trying to avoid making any air pockets. Fold the left corner in toward the centre and then the right corner toward the centre. It should now look like an envelope. Tightly roll the egg roll from the bottom to the top open corner. Press to seal the egg roll together, brushing with a little extra water if need be. Repeat this technique with all 8 egg rolls. 3. Preheat the air fryer to 190ºC. 4. Spray or brush all sides of the egg rolls with mixed vegetables oil. Air fry four egg rolls at a time for 10 minutes, turning them over halfway through the cooking time. 5. Serve hot with duck sauce or your favourite dipping sauce.

Pork and Cabbage Egg Rolls

Prep time: 15 minutes | Cook time: 12 minutes | Makes 12 egg rolls

Cooking oil spray
2 garlic cloves, minced
340 g minced pork
1 teaspoon sesame oil
60 ml soy sauce
2 teaspoons grated peeled fresh
ginger
110 g shredded green cabbage
4 spring onions, green parts (white parts optional), chopped
24 egg roll wrappers

1. Spray a frying pan with the cooking oil and place it over medium-high heat. Add the garlic and cook for 1 minute until fragrant. 2. Add the minced pork to the frying pan. Using a spoon, break the pork into smaller chunks. 3. In a small bowl, whisk the sesame oil, soy sauce, and ginger until combined. Add the sauce to the frying pan. Stir to combine and continue cooking for about 5 minutes until the pork is browned and thoroughly cooked. 4. Stir in the cabbage and spring onions. Transfer the pork mixture to a large bowl. 5. Lay the egg roll wrappers on a flat surface. Dip a basting brush in water and glaze each egg roll wrapper along the edges with the wet brush. This will soften the dough and make it easier to roll. 6. Stack 2 egg roll wrappers (it works best if you double-wrap the egg rolls). Scoop 1 to 2 tablespoons of the pork mixture into the centre of each wrapper stack. 7. Roll one long side of the wrappers up over the filling. Press firmly on the area with the filling, tucking it in lightly to secure it in place. Fold in the left and right sides. Continue rolling to close. Use the basting brush to wet the seam and seal the egg roll. Repeat with the remaining ingredients. 8. Insert the crisper plate into the basket and the basket into the unit. Preheat the unit by selecting AIR FRY, setting the temperature to 200ºC, and setting the time to 3 minutes. Select START/STOP to begin. 9. Once the unit is preheated, spray the crisper plate with cooking oil. Place the egg rolls into the basket. It is okay to stack them. Spray them with cooking oil. 10. Select AIR FRY, set the temperature to 200ºC, and set the time to 12 minutes. Insert the basket into the unit. Select START/STOP to begin. 11. After 8 minutes, use tongs to flip the egg rolls. Reinsert the basket to resume cooking. 12. When the cooking is complete, serve the egg rolls hot.

Kale Chips with Sesame

Prep time: 15 minutes | Cook time: 8 minutes |
Serves 5

2L deribbed kale leaves, torn
into 2-inch pieces
1½ tablespoons olive oil
¾ teaspoon chili powder

¼ teaspoon garlic powder
½ teaspoon paprika
2 teaspoons sesame seeds

1. Preheat air fryer to 180°C. 2. In a large bowl, toss the kale with the olive oil, chili powder, garlic powder, paprika, and sesame seeds until well coated. 3. Put the kale in the air fryer basket and air fry for 8 minutes, flipping the kale twice during cooking, or until the kale is crispy. 4. Serve warm.

Mushroom Tarts

Prep time: 15 minutes | Cook time: 38 minutes |
Makes 15 tarts

2 tablespoons extra-virgin olive
oil, divided
1 small white onion, sliced
227 g shiitake mushrooms,
sliced
¼ teaspoon sea salt
¼ teaspoon freshly ground
black pepper

60 ml dry white wine
1 sheet frozen puff pastry,
thawed
95 g shredded Gruyère cheese
Cooking oil spray
1 tablespoon thinly sliced fresh
chives

1. Insert the crisper plate into the basket and the basket into the unit. Preheat the unit by selecting BAKE, setting the temperature to 150°C, and setting the time to 3 minutes. Select START/STOP to begin. 2. In a heatproof bowl that fits into the basket, stir together 1 tablespoon of olive oil, the onion, and the mushrooms. 3. Once the unit is preheated, place the bowl into the basket. 4. Select BAKE, set the temperature to 150°C, and set the time to 7 minutes. Select START/STOP to begin. 5. After about 2½ minutes, stir the mixed vegetables. Resume cooking. After another 2½ minutes, the mixed vegetables should be browned and tender. Season with the salt and pepper and add the wine. Resume cooking until the liquid evaporates, about 2 minutes. 6. When the cooking is complete, place the bowl on a heatproof surface. 7. Increase the air fryer temperature to 200°C and set the time to 3 minutes. Select START/STOP to begin. 8. Unfold the puff pastry and cut it into 15 (3-by-3-inch) squares. Using a fork, pierce the dough and brush both sides with the remaining 1 tablespoon of olive oil. 9. Evenly distribute half the cheese among the puff pastry squares, leaving a ½-inch border around the edges. Divide the mushroom-onion mixture among the pastry squares and top with the remaining cheese. 10. Once the unit is preheated, spray the crisper plate with cooking oil. Working in batches, place 5 tarts into the basket; do not stack or overlap. 11. Select BAKE, set the temperature to 200°C, and set the time to 8 minutes. Select START/STOP to begin. 12. After 6 minutes, check the tarts; if not yet golden, resume cooking for about 2 minutes more. 13. When the cooking is complete, remove the tarts and transfer to a a wire rack to cool. Repeat steps 10, 11, and 12 with the remaining tarts. 14. Serve garnished with the chives.

Greens Chips with Curried Yoghurt Sauce

Prep time: 10 minutes | Cook time: 5 to 6 minutes |
Serves 4

240 ml low-fat Greek yoghurt
1 tablespoon freshly squeezed
lemon juice
1 tablespoon curry powder
½ bunch curly kale, stemmed,
ribs removed and discarded,

leaves cut into 2- to 3-inch
pieces
½ bunch chard, stemmed, ribs
removed and discarded, leaves
cut into 2- to 3-inch pieces
1½ teaspoons olive oil

1. In a small bowl, stir together the yoghurt, lemon juice, and curry powder. Set aside. 2. In a large bowl, toss the kale and chard with the olive oil, working the oil into the leaves with your hands. This helps break up the fibres in the leaves so the chips are tender. 3. Air fry the greens in batches at 200°C for 5 to 6 minutes, until crisp, shaking the basket once during cooking. Serve with the yoghurt sauce.

Cinnamon-Apple Crisps

Prep time: 10 minutes | Cook time: 32 minutes |
Serves 4

Oil, for spraying
2 Red Delicious or Honeycrisp
apples

¼ teaspoon cinnamon powder,
divided

1. Line the air fryer basket with baking paper and spray lightly with oil. 2. Trim the uneven ends off the apples. Using a mandoline on the thinnest setting or a sharp knife, cut the apples into very thin slices. Discard the cores. 3. Place half of the apple slices in a single layer in the prepared basket and sprinkle with half of the cinnamon. 4. Place a metal fryer trivet on top of the apples to keep them from flying around while they are cooking. 5. Air fry at 150°C for 16 minutes, flipping every 5 minutes to ensure even cooking. Repeat with the remaining apple slices and cinnamon. 6. Let cool to at room temperature before serving. The crisps will firm up as they cool.

Parmesan Chips

Prep time: 10 minutes | Cook time: 15 minutes per batch | Serves 2

2 to 3 large russet potatoes or Maris Piper potatoes, peeled and cut into ½-inch sticks
2 teaspoons mixed vegetables or rapeseed oil
50 g grated Parmesan cheese

½ teaspoon salt
Freshly ground black pepper, to taste
1 teaspoon fresh chopped parsley

1. Bring a large saucepan of salted water to a boil on the hop while you peel and cut the potatoes. Blanch the potatoes in the boiling salted water for 4 minutes while you preheat the air fryer to 200ºC. Strain the potatoes and rinse them with cold water. Dry them well with a clean kitchen towel. 2. Toss the dried potato sticks gently with the oil and place them in the air fryer basket. Air fry for 25 minutes, shaking the basket a few times while the fries cook to help them brown evenly. 3. Combine the Parmesan cheese, salt and pepper. With 2 minutes left on the air fryer cooking time, sprinkle the fries with the Parmesan cheese mixture. Toss the fries to coat them evenly with the cheese mixture and continue to air fry for the final 2 minutes, until the cheese has melted and just starts to brown. Sprinkle the finished fries with chopped parsley, a little more grated Parmesan cheese if you like, and serve.

Polenta Fries with Chilli-Lime Mayo

Prep time: 10 minutes | Cook time: 28 minutes | Serves 4

Polenta Fries:
2 teaspoons mixed vegetables or olive oil
¼ teaspoon paprika
450 g prepared polenta, cut into 3-inch × ½-inch strips
Chilli-Lime Mayo:
120 ml mayonnaise

1 teaspoon chili powder
1 teaspoon finely chopped fresh coriander
¼ teaspoon cumin powder
Juice of ½ lime
Salt and freshly ground black pepper, to taste

1. Preheat the air fryer to 200ºC. 2. Mix the oil and paprika in a bowl. Add the polenta strips and toss until evenly coated. 3. Transfer the polenta strips to the air fry basket and air fry for 28 minutes until the fries are golden, shaking the basket once during cooking. Season as desired with salt and pepper. 4. Meanwhile, whisk together all the ingredients for the chilli-lime mayo in a small bowl. 5. Remove the polenta fries from the air fryer to a plate and serve alongside the chilli-lime mayo as a dipping sauce.

Stuffed Figs with Goat Cheese and Honey

Prep time: 5 minutes | Cook time: 10 minutes | Serves 4

8 fresh figs
57 g goat cheese
¼ teaspoon cinnamon powder

1 tablespoon honey, plus more for serving
1 tablespoon olive oil

1. Preheat the air fryer to 180ºC. Line an 8-by-8-inch baking dish with baking paper paper that comes up the side so you can lift it out after cooking. 2. In a large bowl, mix together all of the ingredients until well combined. 3. Press the oat mixture into the pan in an even layer. 4. Place the pan into the air fryer basket and bake for 15 minutes. 5. Remove the pan from the air fryer and lift the granola cake out of the pan using the edges of the baking paper paper. 6. Allow to cool for 5 minutes before slicing into 6 equal bars. 7. Serve immediately or wrap in plastic wrap and store at room temperature for up to 1 week.

Egg Roll Pizza Sticks

Prep time: 10 minutes | Cook time: 5 minutes | Serves 4

Olive oil
8 pieces low-fat string cheese
8 egg roll wrappers or spring roll pastry

24 slices turkey pepperoni or salami
Marinara sauce, for dipping (optional)

1. Spray the air fryer basket lightly with olive oil. Fill a small bowl with water. 2. Place each egg roll wrapper diagonally on a work surface. It should look like a diamond. 3. Place 3 slices of turkey pepperoni in a vertical line down the centre of the wrapper. 4. Place 1 mozzarella cheese cheese stick on top of the turkey pepperoni. 5. Fold the top and bottom corners of the egg roll wrapper over the cheese stick. 6. Fold the left corner over the cheese stick and roll the cheese stick up to resemble a spring roll. Dip a finger in the water and seal the edge of the roll 7. Repeat with the rest of the pizza sticks. 8. Place them in the air fryer basket in a single layer, making sure to leave a little space between each one. Lightly spray the pizza sticks with oil. You may need to cook these in batches. 9. Air fry at 190ºC until the pizza sticks are lightly browned and crispy, about 5 minutes. 10. These are best served hot while the cheese is melted. Accompany with a small bowl of marinara sauce, if desired.

Easy Roasted Chickpeas

Prep time: 5 minutes | Cook time: 15 minutes | Makes about 240 ml

1 (425 g) can chickpeas, drained
2 teaspoons curry powder

¼ teaspoon salt
1 tablespoon olive oil

1. Drain chickpeas thoroughly and spread in a single layer on kitchen roll. Cover with another paper towel and press gently to remove extra moisture. Don't press too hard or you'll crush the chickpeas. 2. Mix curry powder and salt together. 3. Place chickpeas in a medium-sized bowl and sprinkle with seasonings. Stir well to coat. 4. Add olive oil and stir again to distribute oil. 5. Air fry at 200°C for 15 minutes, stopping to shake basket about halfway through cooking time. 6. Cool completely and store in airtight container.

Old Bay Chicken Wings

Prep time: 10 minutes | Cook time: 12 to 15 minutes | Serves 4

2 tablespoons Old Bay or all-purpose seasoning
2 teaspoons baking powder
2 teaspoons salt

900 g chicken wings, patted dry
Cooking spray

1. Preheat the air fryer to 200°C. Lightly spray the air fryer basket with cooking spray. 2. Combine the seasoning, baking powder, and salt in a large zip-top plastic bag. Add the chicken wings, seal, and shake until the wings are thoroughly coated in the seasoning mixture. 3. Lay the chicken wings in the air fryer basket in a single layer and lightly mist with cooking spray. You may need to work in batches to avoid overcrowding. 4. Air fry for 12 to 15 minutes, flipping the wings halfway through, or until the wings are lightly browned and the internal temperature reaches at least 74°C on a meat thermometer. 5. Remove from the basket to a plate and repeat with the remaining chicken wings. 6. Serve hot.

Ranch Oyster Snack Crackers

Prep time: 3 minutes | Cook time: 12 minutes | Serves 6

Oil, for spraying
60 ml olive oil
2 teaspoons dry ranch dressing mix
1 teaspoon chili powder

½ teaspoon dried fresh dill weed
½ teaspoon garlic powder
½ teaspoon salt
1 (255 g) bag water biscuits or low-salt biscuits

1. Preheat the air fryer to 160°C. Line the air fryer basket with baking paper and spray lightly with oil. 2. In a large bowl, mix together the olive oil, ranch dressing mix, chili powder, fresh dill, garlic, and salt. Add the crackers and toss until evenly coated. 3. Place the mixture in the prepared basket. 4. Cook for 10 to 12 minutes, shaking or stirring every 3 to 4 minutes, or until crisp and golden.

Chapter 6 Family Favorites

Pecan Rolls

Prep time: 20 minutes | Cook time: 20 to 24 minutes | Makes 12 rolls

220 g plain flour, plus more for dusting	180 ml milk, whole or semi-skimmed
2 tablespoons caster sugar, plus 60 ml, divided	40 g packed light muscovado sugar
1 teaspoon salt	120g chopped pecans, toasted
3 tablespoons butter, at room temperature	1 to 2 tablespoons oil
	35g icing sugar (optional)

1. In a large bowl, whisk the flour, 2 tablespoons caster sugar, and salt until blended. 2.Stir in the butter and milk briefly until a sticky dough form. In a small bowl, stir together the brown sugar and remaining 60 g caster sugar. 3.Place a piece of parchment paper on a work surface and dust it with flour. Roll the dough on the prepared surface to ¼ inch thickness. 4.Spread the sugar mixture over the dough. Sprinkle the pecans on top. Roll up the dough jelly roll-style, pinching the ends to seal. 5.Cut the dough into 12 rolls. Preheat the air fryer to 160ºC. 6.Line the air fryer basket with parchment paper and spritz the parchment with oil. Place 6 rolls on the prepared parchment. Bake for 5 minutes. 7.Flip the rolls and bake for 5 to 7 minutes more until lightly browned. Repeat with the remaining rolls. 8.Sprinkle with icing sugar (if using).

Fish and Vegetable Tacos

Prep time: 15 minutes | Cook time: 9 to 12 minutes | Serves 4

450 g white fish fillets, such as sole or cod	1 large carrot, grated
2 teaspoons olive oil	120 ml low-salt salsa
3 tablespoons freshly squeezed lemon juice, divided	80 ml low-fat Greek yoghurt
350 g chopped red cabbage	4 soft low-salt wholemeal tortillas

1. Brush the fish with the olive oil and sprinkle with 1 tablespoon of lemon juice. 2.Air fry in the air fryer basket at 200ºC for 9 to 12 minutes, or until the fish just flakes when tested with a fork. 3.Meanwhile, in a medium bowl, stir together the remaining 2 tablespoons of lemon juice, the red cabbage, carrot, salsa, and yoghurt. 4.When the fish is cooked, remove it from the air fryer basket and break it up into large pieces. 5.Offer the fish, tortillas, and the cabbage mixture, and let each person assemble a taco.

Berry Cheesecake

Prep time: 5 minutes | Cook time: 10 minutes | Serves 4

Oil, for spraying	1 large egg
227 g soft white cheese	½ teaspoon vanilla extract
6 tablespoons sugar	¼ teaspoon lemon juice
1 tablespoon sour cream	120 g fresh mixed berries

1. Preheat the air fryer to 180ºC. 2.Line the air fryer basket with parchment and spray lightly with oil. 3.In a blender, combine the soft white cheese, sugar, sour cream, egg, vanilla, and lemon juice and blend until smooth. 4.Pour the mixture into a 4-inch springform pan. 5.Place the pan in the prepared basket. Cook for 8 to 10 minutes, or until only the very centre jiggles slightly when the pan is moved. 6.Refrigerate the cheesecake in the pan for at least 2 hours. 7.Release the sides from the springform pan, top the cheesecake with the mixed berries, and serve.

Mixed Berry Crumble

Prep time: 10 minutes | Cook time: 11 to 16 minutes | Serves 4

120 g chopped fresh strawberries	1 tablespoon honey
120 g fresh blueberries	80 g wholemeal plain flour
80 g frozen raspberries	3 tablespoons light muscovado sugar
1 tablespoon freshly squeezed lemon juice	2 tablespoons unsalted butter, melted

1. In a baking pan, combine the strawberries, blueberries, and raspberries. 2.Drizzle with the lemon juice and honey. 3.In a small bowl, mix the pastry flour and brown sugar. 4.Stir in the butter and mix until crumbly. 5.Sprinkle this mixture over the fruit. 6.Bake at 190ºC for 11 to 16 minutes, or until the fruit is tender and bubbly and the topping is golden brown. 7.Serve warm.

Pork Burgers with Red Cabbage Salad

Prep time: 20 minutes | Cook time: 7 to 9 minutes | Serves 4

120 ml Greek yoghurt	450 g lean finely chopped pork
2 tablespoons low-salt mustard, divided	½ teaspoon paprika
1 tablespoon lemon juice	235 g mixed salad leaves
60 g sliced red cabbage	2 small tomatoes, sliced
60 g grated carrots	8 small low-salt wholemeal sandwich buns, cut in half

1. In a small bowl, combine the yoghurt, 1 tablespoon mustard, lemon juice, cabbage, and carrots; mix and refrigerate. 2.In a medium bowl, combine the pork, remaining 1 tablespoon mustard, and paprika. Form into 8 small patties. Put the sliders into the air fryer basket. 3.Air fry at 200°C for 7 to 9 minutes, or until the sliders register 74°C as tested with a meat thermometer. 4.Assemble the burgers by placing some of the lettuce greens on a bun bottom. 5.Top with a tomato slice, the burgers, and the cabbage mixture. 6.Add the bun top and serve immediately.

Meringue Cookies

Prep time: 15 minutes | Cook time: 1 hour 30 minutes | Makes 20 cookies

Oil, for spraying	185 g sugar
4 large egg whites	Pinch cream of tartar

1. Preheat the air fryer to 60°C. 2.Line the air fryer basket with parchment and spray lightly with oil. 3.In a small heatproof bowl, whisk together the egg whites and sugar. 4.Fill a small saucepan halfway with water, place it over medium heat, and bring to a light simmer. 5.Place the bowl with the egg whites on the saucepan, making sure the bottom of the bowl does not touch the water. 6.Whisk the mixture until the sugar is dissolved. Transfer the mixture to a large bowl and add the cream of tartar. 7.Using an electric mixer, beat the mixture on high until it is glossy and stiff peaks form. 8.Transfer the mixture to a piping bag or a zip-top plastic bag with a corner cut off. Pipe rounds into the prepared basket. 9.You may need to work in batches, depending on the size of your air fryer. Cook for 1 hour 30 minutes. 10.Turn off the air fryer and let the meringues cool completely inside. 11.The residual heat will continue to dry them out.

Old Bay Tilapia

Prep time: 15 minutes | Cook time: 6 minutes | Serves 4

Oil, for spraying	½ teaspoon salt
235 ml panko breadcrumbs	¼ teaspoon freshly ground black pepper
2 tablespoons Old Bay or all-purpose seasoning	1 large egg
2 teaspoons granulated garlic	4 tilapia fillets
1 teaspoon onion powder	

Preheat the air fryer to 204°C. Line the air fryer basket with parchment and spray lightly with oil. In a shallow bowl, mix together the breadcrumbs, seasoning, garlic, onion powder, salt, and black pepper. In a small bowl, whisk the egg. Coat the tilapia in the egg, then dredge in the bread crumb mixture until completely coated. Place the tilapia in the prepared basket. You may need to work in batches, depending on the size of your air fryer. Spray lightly with oil. Cook for 4 to 6 minutes, depending on the thickness of the fillets, until the internal temperature reaches 64°C. Serve immediately.

Fried Green Tomatoes

Prep time: 15 minutes | Cook time: 6 to 8 minutes | Serves 4

4 medium green tomatoes	120 g Japanese breadcrumbs
50 g plain flour	2 teaspoons olive oil
2 egg whites	1 teaspoon paprika
60 ml almond milk	1 clove garlic, minced
235 g ground almonds	

1. Rinse the tomatoes and pat dry. 2.Cut the tomatoes into ½-inch slices, discarding the thinner ends. Put the flour on a plate. 3.In a shallow bowl, beat the egg whites with the almond milk until frothy. 4.And on another plate, combine the almonds, breadcrumbs, olive oil, paprika, and garlic and mix well. 5.Dip the tomato slices into the flour, then into the egg white mixture, then into the almond mixture to coat. 6.Place four of the coated tomato slices in the air fryer basket. 7.Air fry at 200°C for 6 to 8 minutes or until the tomato coating is crisp and golden brown. 8.Repeat with remaining tomato slices and serve immediately.

Cheesy Roasted Sweet Potatoes

Prep time: 7 minutes | Cook time: 18 to 23 minutes | Serves 4

2 large sweet potatoes, peeled and sliced
1 teaspoon olive oil
1 tablespoon white balsamic vinegar

1 teaspoon dried thyme
60 g Parmesan cheese

1. In a large bowl, drizzle the sweet potato slices with the olive oil and toss. 2.Sprinkle with the balsamic vinegar and thyme and toss again. 3.Sprinkle the potatoes with the Parmesan cheese and toss to coat. 4.Roast the slices, in batches, in the air fryer basket at 200°C for 18 to 23 minutes, tossing the sweet potato slices in the basket once during cooking, until tender. 5.Repeat with the remaining sweet potato slices. 6.Serve immediately.

Beef Jerky

Prep time: 30 minutes | Cook time: 2 hours | Serves 8

Oil, for spraying
450 g silverside, cut into thin, short slices
60 ml soy sauce
3 tablespoons packed light muscovado sugar

1 tablespoon minced garlic
1 teaspoon ground ginger
1 tablespoon water

1. Line the air fryer basket with parchment and spray lightly with oil. 2.Place the steak, soy sauce, brown sugar, garlic, ginger, and water in a zip-top plastic bag, seal, and shake well until evenly coated. 3.Refrigerate for 30 minutes. Place the steak in the prepared basket in a single layer. 4.You may need to work in batches, depending on the size of your air fryer. 5.Air fry at 80°C for at least 2 hours. 6.Add more time if you like your jerky a bit tougher.

Chapter 7 Fast and Easy Everyday Favourites

Chapter 7 Fast and Easy Everyday Favourites

Cheesy Jalapeño Cornbread

Prep time: 10 minutes | Cook time: 20 minutes |

Serves 8

160 ml cornmeal
80 ml plain flour
¾ teaspoon baking powder
2 tablespoons margarine, melted
½ teaspoon rock salt
1 tablespoon granulated sugar

180 ml whole milk
1 large egg, beaten
1 jalapeño pepper, thinly sliced
80 ml shredded extra mature Cheddar cheese
Cooking spray

1. Preheat the air fryer to 152ºC. Spritz the air fryer basket with cooking spray. 2.Combine all the ingredients in a large bowl. Stir to mix well. Pour the mixture in a baking pan. 3.Arrange the pan in the preheated air fryer. Bake for 20 minutes or until a toothpick inserted in the centre of the bread comes out clean. 4.When the cooking is complete, remove the baking pan from the air fryer and allow the bread to cool for a few minutes before slicing to serve.

Sweet Corn and Carrot Fritters

Prep time: 10 minutes | Cook time: 8 to 11 minutes |

Serves 4

1 medium-sized carrot, grated
1 yellow onion, finely chopped
4 ounces (113 g) canned sweet corn kernels, drained
1 teaspoon sea salt flakes
1 tablespoon chopped fresh cilantro

1 medium-sized egg, whisked
2 tablespoons plain milk
1 cup grated Parmesan cheese
¼ cup flour
⅓ teaspoon baking powder
⅓ teaspoon sugar
Cooking spray

1. Preheat the air fryer to 350ºF (177ºC). 2. Place the grated carrot in a colander and press down to squeeze out any excess moisture. Dry it with a paper towel. 3. Combine the carrots with the remaining ingredients. 4. Mold 1 tablespoon of the mixture into a ball and press it down with your hand or a spoon to flatten it. Repeat until the rest of the mixture is used up. 5. Spritz the balls

with cooking spray. 6. Arrange in the air fryer basket, taking care not to overlap any balls. Bake for 8 to 11 minutes, or until they're firm. 7. Serve warm.

Baked Cheese Sandwich

Prep time: 5 minutes | Cook time: 8 minutes | Serves 2

2 tablespoons mayonnaise
4 thick slices sourdough bread
4 thick slices Brie cheese

8 slices hot capicola or prosciutto

1. Preheat the air fryer to 180ºC. 2.Spread the mayonnaise on one side of each slice of bread. 3.Place 2 slices of bread in the air fryer basket, mayonnaise-side down. 4.Place the slices of Brie and capicola on the bread and cover with the remaining two slices of bread, mayonnaise-side up. 5.Bake for 8 minutes, or until the cheese has melted. 6.Serve immediately.

Beetroot Salad with Lemon Vinaigrette

Prep time: 10 minutes | Cook time: 12 to 15 minutes | Serves 4

6 medium red and golden beetroots, peeled and sliced
1 teaspoon olive oil
¼ teaspoon rock salt
120 g crumbled feta cheese
2 kg mixed greens

Cooking spray
Vinaigrette:
2 teaspoons olive oil
2 tablespoons chopped fresh chives
Juice of 1 lemon

1. Preheat the air fryer to 180ºC. 2.In a large bowl, toss the beetroots, olive oil, and rock salt. 3.Spray the air fryer basket with cooking spray, then place the beetroots in the basket and air fry for 12 to 15 minutes or until tender. 4.While the beetroots cook, make the vinaigrette in a large bowl by whisking together the olive oil, lemon juice, and chives. 5.Remove the beetroots from the air fryer, toss in the vinaigrette, and allow to cool for 5 minutes. 6.Add the feta and serve on top of the mixed greens.

Bacon Pinwheels

**Prep time: 10 minutes | Cook time: 10 minutes |
Makes 8 pinwheels**

1 sheet puff pastry
2 tablespoons maple syrup
48 g brown sugar

8 slices bacon
Ground black pepper, to taste
Cooking spray

Preheat the air fryer to 180ºC. Spritz the air fryer basket with cooking spray. Roll the puff pastry into a 10-inch square with a rolling pin on a clean work surface, then cut the pastry into 8 strips. Brush the strips with maple syrup and sprinkle with sugar, leaving a 1-inch far end uncovered. Arrange each slice of bacon on each strip, leaving a ⅛-inch length of bacon hang over the end close to you. Sprinkle with black pepper. From the end close to you, roll the strips into pinwheels, then dab the uncovered end with water and seal the rolls. Arrange the pinwheels in the preheated air fryer and spritz with cooking spray. Air fry for 10 minutes or until golden brown. Flip the pinwheels halfway through. Serve immediately.

Air Fried Broccoli

Prep time: 5 minutes | Cook time: 6 minutes | Serves 1

4 egg yolks
60 g melted butter
240 g coconut flour

Salt and pepper, to taste
475 g broccoli florets

1. Preheat the air fryer to 200ºC. In a bowl, whisk the egg yolks and melted butter together. 2.Throw in the coconut flour, salt and pepper, then stir again to combine well. 3.Dip each broccoli floret into the mixture and place in the air fryer basket. 4.Air fry for 6 minutes in batches if necessary. Take care when removing them from the air fryer and serve immediately.

Cheesy Potato Patties

**Prep time: 5 minutes | Cook time: 10 minutes |
Serves 8**

900 g white potatoes
120 g finely chopped spring
onions
½ teaspoon freshly ground
black pepper, or more to taste
1 tablespoon fine sea salt

½ teaspoon hot paprika
475 g shredded Colby or
Monterey Jack cheese
60 ml rapeseed oil
235 g crushed crackers

1. Preheat the air fryer to 180ºC. Boil the potatoes until soft. 2.Dry them off and peel them before mashing thoroughly, leaving no lumps. 3.Combine the mashed potatoes with spring onions, pepper, salt, paprika, and cheese. 4.Mould the mixture into balls with your hands and press with your palm to flatten them into patties. 5.In a shallow dish, combine the rapeseed oil and crushed crackers. 6.Coat the patties in the crumb mixture. 7.Bake the patties for about 10 minutes, in multiple batches if necessary. 8.Serve hot.

Air Fried Butternut Squash with Chopped Hazelnuts

**Prep time: 10 minutes | Cook time: 20 minutes |
Makes 700 ml**

2 tablespoons whole hazelnuts
700 g butternut squash, peeled,
deseeded, and cubed
¼ teaspoon rock salt

¼ teaspoon freshly ground
black pepper
2 teaspoons olive oil
Cooking spray

1. Preheat the air fryer to 150ºC. 2.Spritz the air fryer basket with cooking spray. 3.Arrange the hazelnuts in the preheated air fryer. Air fry for 3 minutes or until soft. 4.Chopped the hazelnuts roughly and transfer to a small bowl. Set aside. 5.Set the air fryer temperature to 180ºC. 6.Spritz with cooking spray. Put the butternut squash in a large bowl, then sprinkle with salt and pepper and drizzle with olive oil. 7.Toss to coat well. Transfer the squash in the air fryer. Air fry for 20 minutes or until the squash is soft. 8.Shake the basket halfway through the frying time. 9.When the frying is complete, transfer the squash onto a plate and sprinkle with chopped hazelnuts before serving.

Rosemary and Orange Roasted Chickpeas

**Prep time: 5 minutes | Cook time: 10 to 12 minutes |
Makes 1 L**

1 kg cooked chickpeas
2 tablespoons vegetable oil
1 teaspoon rock salt
1 teaspoon cumin

1 teaspoon paprika
Zest of 1 orange
1 tablespoon chopped fresh
rosemary

1. Preheat the air fryer to 200ºC. 2.Make sure the chickpeas are completely dry prior to roasting. In a medium bowl, toss the chickpeas with oil, salt, cumin, and paprika. 3.Working in batches, spread the chickpeas in a single layer in the air fryer basket. 4.Air fry for 10 to 12 minutes until crisp, shaking once halfway through. 5.Return the warm chickpeas to the bowl and toss with the orange zest and rosemary. 6.Allow to cool completely. Serve.

Simple Pea Delight

Prep time: 5 minutes | Cook time: 15 minutes |
Serves 2 to 4

120 g flour
1 teaspoon baking powder
3 eggs
235 ml coconut milk
235 g soft white cheese
3 tablespoons pea protein
120 g chicken or turkey strips
Pinch of sea salt
235 g Mozzarella cheese

1. Preheat the air fryer to 200°C. 2.In a large bowl, mix all ingredients together using a large wooden spoon. 3.Spoon equal amounts of the mixture into muffin cups and bake for 15 minutes. 4.Serve immediately.

Scalloped Veggie Mix

Prep time: 10 minutes | Cook time: 15 minutes |
Serves 4

1 Yukon Gold or other small white potato, thinly sliced
1 small sweet potato, peeled and thinly sliced
1 medium carrot, thinly sliced
60 g minced onion
3 garlic cloves, minced
180 ml 2 percent milk
2 tablespoons cornflour
½ teaspoon dried thyme

1. Preheat the air fryer to 190°C. 2.In a baking tray, layer the potato, sweet potato, carrot, onion, and garlic. 3.In a small bowl, whisk the milk, cornflour, and thyme until blended. 4.Pour the milk mixture evenly over the vegetables in the pan. Bake for 15 minutes. 5.Check the casserole—it should be golden brown on top, and the vegetables should be tender. 6.Serve immediately.

Spinach and Carrot Balls

Prep time: 10 minutes | Cook time: 10 minutes |
Serves 4

2 slices toasted bread
1 carrot, peeled and grated
1 package fresh spinach, blanched and chopped
½ onion, chopped
1 egg, beaten
½ teaspoon garlic powder
1 teaspoon minced garlic
1 teaspoon salt
½ teaspoon black pepper
1 tablespoon Engevita yeast flakes
1 tablespoon flour

1. Preheat the air fryer to 200°C. 2.In a food processor, pulse the toasted bread to form breadcrumbs. 3.Transfer into a shallow dish or bowl. In a bowl, mix together all the other ingredients. 4.Use your hands to shape the mixture into small-sized balls. 5.Roll the balls in the breadcrumbs, ensuring to cover them well. 6.Put in the air fryer basket and air fry for 10 minutes. 7.Serve immediately.

Traditional Queso Fundido

Prep time: 10 minutes | Cook time: 25 minutes |
Serves 4

110 g fresh Mexican (or Spanish if unavailable) chorizo, casings removed
1 medium onion, chopped
3 cloves garlic, minced
235 g chopped tomato
2 jalapeños, deseeded and diced
2 teaspoons ground cumin
475 g shredded Oaxaca or Mozzarella cheese
120 ml half-and-half (60 g whole milk and 60 ml cream combined)
Celery sticks or tortilla chips, for serving

1. Preheat the air fryer to 200°C. 2.In a baking tray, combine the chorizo, onion, garlic, tomato, jalapeños, and cumin. Stir to combine. 3.Place the pan in the air fryer basket. 4.Air fry for 15 minutes, or until the sausage is cooked, stirring halfway through the cooking time to break up the sausage. 5.Add the cheese and half-and-half; stir to combine. 6.Air fry for 10 minutes, or until the cheese has melted. 7.Serve with celery sticks or tortilla chips.

Baked Chorizo Scotch Eggs

Prep time:5 minutes | Cook time: 15 to 20 minutes |
Makes 4 eggs

450 g Mexican chorizo or other seasoned sausage meat
4 soft-boiled eggs plus 1 raw egg
1 tablespoon water
120 ml plain flour
235 ml panko breadcrumbs
Cooking spray

1. Divide the chorizo into 4 equal portions. Flatten each portion into a disc. Place a soft-boiled egg in the centre of each disc. Wrap the chorizo around the egg, encasing it completely. Place the encased eggs on a plate and chill for at least 30 minutes. 2.Preheat the air fryer to 182°C. 3.Beat the raw egg with 1 tablespoon of water. Place the flour on a small plate and the panko on a second plate. Working with 1 egg at a time, roll the encased egg in the flour, then dip it in the egg mixture. Dredge the egg in the panko and place on a plate. Repeat with the remaining eggs. 4.Spray the eggs with oil and place in the air fryer basket. Bake for 10 minutes. Turn and bake for an additional 5 to 10 minutes, or until browned and crisp on all sides. 5.Serve immediately.

Beef Bratwursts

4 (85 g) beef bratwursts

1. Preheat the air fryer to 190ºC. Place the beef bratwursts in the air fryer basket and air fry for 15 minutes, turning once halfway through. Serve hot.

Chapter 8 Vegetables and Sides

Chapter 8 Vegetables and Sides

Crispy Lemon Artichoke Hearts

Prep time: 10 minutes | Cook time: 15 minutes |
Serves 2

1 (425 g) can artichoke hearts in water, drained
1 egg
1 tablespoon water
30 g whole wheat bread crumbs
¼ teaspoon salt
¼ teaspoon paprika
½ lemon

1. Preheat the air fryer to 190°C. 2. In a medium shallow bowl, beat together the egg and water until frothy. 3. In a separate medium shallow bowl, mix together the bread crumbs, salt, and paprika. 4. Dip each artichoke heart into the egg mixture, then into the bread crumb mixture, coating the outside with the crumbs. Place the artichokes hearts in a single layer of the air fryer basket. 5. Fry the artichoke hearts for 15 minutes. 6. Remove the artichokes from the air fryer, and squeeze fresh lemon juice over the top before serving.

Spinach and Cheese Stuffed Tomatoes

Prep time: 20 minutes | Cook time: 15 minutes |
Serves 2

4 ripe beefsteak tomatoes
¾ teaspoon black pepper
½ teaspoon coarse sea salt
1 (280 g) package frozen chopped spinach, thawed and squeezed dry
1 (150 g) package garlic-and-herb Boursin cheese
3 tablespoons sour cream
45 g finely grated Parmesan cheese

1. Cut the tops off the tomatoes. Using a small spoon, carefully remove and discard the pulp. Season the insides with ½ teaspoon of the black pepper and ¼ teaspoon of the salt. Invert the tomatoes onto paper towels and allow to drain while you make the filling. 2. Meanwhile, in a medium bowl, combine the spinach, Boursin cheese, sour cream, ½ of the Parmesan, and the remaining ¼ teaspoon salt and ¼ teaspoon pepper. Stir until ingredients are well combined. Divide the filling among the tomatoes. Top with the remaining ½ of the Parmesan. 3. Place the tomatoes in the air fryer basket. Set the air fryer to 180°C for 15 minutes, or until the filling is hot.

Sweet and Crispy Roasted Pearl Onions

Prep time: 5 minutes | Cook time: 18 minutes |
Serves 3

1 (410 g) package frozen pearl onions (do not thaw)
2 tablespoons extra-virgin olive oil
2 tablespoons balsamic vinegar
2 teaspoons finely chopped fresh rosemary
½ teaspoon coarse sea salt
¼ teaspoon black pepper

1. In a medium bowl, combine the onions, olive oil, vinegar, rosemary, salt, and pepper until well coated. 2. Transfer the onions to the air fryer basket. Set the air fryer to 200°C for 18 minutes, or until the onions are tender and lightly charred, stirring once or twice during the cooking time.

Cauliflower Rice Balls

Prep time: 10 minutes | Cook time: 8 minutes |
Serves 4

1 (280 g) steamer bag cauliflower rice, cooked according to package instructions
110 g shredded Mozzarella cheese
1 large egg
60 g plain pork scratchings, finely crushed
¼ teaspoon salt
½ teaspoon Italian seasoning

1. Place cauliflower into a large bowl and mix with Mozzarella. 2. Whisk egg in a separate medium bowl. Place pork scratchings into another large bowl with salt and Italian seasoning. 3. Separate cauliflower mixture into four equal sections and form each into a ball. Carefully dip a ball into whisked egg, then roll in pork scratchings. Repeat with remaining balls. 4. Place cauliflower balls into ungreased air fryer basket. Adjust the temperature to 200°C and air fry for 8 minutes. Rice balls will be golden when done. 5. Use a spatula to carefully move cauliflower balls to a large dish for serving. Serve warm.

Crispy Green Beans

Prep time: 5 minutes | Cook time: 8 minutes | Serves 4

2 teaspoons olive oil
230 g fresh green beans, ends trimmed

¼ teaspoon salt
¼ teaspoon ground black pepper

1. In a large bowl, drizzle olive oil over green beans and sprinkle with salt and pepper. 2. Place green beans into ungreased air fryer basket. Adjust the temperature to 180°C and set the timer for 8 minutes, shaking the basket two times during cooking. Green beans will be dark golden and crispy at the edges when done. Serve warm.

Spiced Honey-Walnut Carrots

Prep time: 5 minutes | Cook time: 12 minutes | Serves 6

450 g baby carrots
2 tablespoons olive oil
80 g raw honey

¼ teaspoon ground cinnamon
25 g black walnuts, chopped

1. Preheat the air fryer to 180°C. 2. In a large bowl, toss the baby carrots with olive oil, honey, and cinnamon until well coated. 3. Pour into the air fryer and roast for 6 minutes. Shake the basket, sprinkle the walnuts on top, and roast for 6 minutes more. 4. Remove the carrots from the air fryer and serve.

Indian Aubergine Bharta

Prep time: 15 minutes | Cook time: 20 minutes | Serves 4

1 medium aubergine
2 tablespoons vegetable oil
25 g finely minced onion
100 g finely chopped fresh tomato

2 tablespoons fresh lemon juice
2 tablespoons chopped fresh coriander
½ teaspoon coarse sea salt
⅛ teaspoon cayenne pepper

1. Rub the aubergine all over with the vegetable oil. Place the aubergine in the air fryer basket. Set the air fryer to 200°C for 20 minutes, or until the aubergine skin is blistered and charred. 2. Transfer the aubergine to a re-sealable plastic bag, seal, and set aside for 15 to 20 minutes (the aubergine will finish cooking in the residual heat trapped in the bag). 3. Transfer the aubergine to a large bowl. Peel off and discard the charred skin. Roughly mash the aubergine flesh. Add the onion, tomato, lemon juice, coriander, salt, and cayenne. Stir to combine.

Chermoula-Roasted Beetroots

Prep time: 15 minutes | Cook time: 25 minutes | Serves 4

Chermoula:
30 g packed fresh coriander leaves
15 g packed fresh parsley leaves
6 cloves garlic, peeled
2 teaspoons smoked paprika
2 teaspoons ground cumin
1 teaspoon ground coriander
½ to 1 teaspoon cayenne pepper
Pinch crushed saffron (optional)

115 g extra-virgin olive oil
coarse sea salt, to taste
Beetroots:
3 medium beetroots, trimmed, peeled, and cut into 1-inch chunks
2 tablespoons chopped fresh coriander
2 tablespoons chopped fresh parsley

1. For the chermoula: In a food processor, combine the fresh coriander, parsley, garlic, paprika, cumin, ground coriander, and cayenne. Pulse until coarsely chopped. Add the saffron, if using, and process until combined. With the food processor running, slowly add the olive oil in a steady stream; process until the sauce is uniform. Season to taste with salt. 2. For the beetroots: In a large bowl, drizzle the beetroots with ½ cup of the chermoula, or enough to coat. Arrange the beetroots in the air fryer basket. Set the air fryer to 190°C for 25 to minutes, or until the beetroots are tender. 3. Transfer the beetroots to a serving platter. Sprinkle with chopped coriander and parsley and serve.

Broccoli with Sesame Dressing

Prep time: 5 minutes | Cook time: 10 minutes | Serves 4

425 g broccoli florets, cut into bite-size pieces
1 tablespoon olive oil
¼ teaspoon salt
2 tablespoons sesame seeds
2 tablespoons rice vinegar

2 tablespoons coconut aminos
2 tablespoons sesame oil
½ teaspoon xylitol
¼ teaspoon red pepper flakes (optional)

1. Preheat the air fryer to 200°C. 2. In a large bowl, toss the broccoli with the olive oil and salt until thoroughly coated. 3. Transfer the broccoli to the air fryer basket. Pausing halfway through the cooking time to shake the basket, air fry for 10 minutes until the stems are tender and the edges are beginning to crisp. 4. Meanwhile, in the same large bowl, whisk together the sesame seeds, vinegar, coconut aminos, sesame oil, xylitol, and red pepper flakes (if using). 5. Transfer the broccoli to the bowl and toss until thoroughly coated with the seasonings. Serve warm or at room temperature.

Southwestern Roasted Corn

Prep time: 10 minutes | Cook time: 10 minutes | Serves 4

Corn:

240 g thawed frozen corn kernels

50 g diced yellow onion

150 g mixed diced bell peppers

1 jalapeño, diced

1 tablespoon fresh lemon juice

1 teaspoon ground cumin

½ teaspoon ancho chili powder

½ teaspoon coarse sea salt

For Serving:

150 g queso fresco or feta cheese

10 g chopped fresh coriander

1 tablespoon fresh lemon juice

1. For the corn: In a large bowl, stir together the corn, onion, bell peppers, jalapeño, lemon juice, cumin, chili powder, and salt until well incorporated. 2. Pour the spiced vegetables into the air fryer basket. Set the air fryer to 190ºC for 10 minutes, stirring halfway through the cooking time. 3. Transfer the corn mixture to a serving bowl. Add the cheese, coriander, and lemon juice and stir well to combine. Serve immediately.

Potato with Creamy Cheese

Prep time: 5 minutes | Cook time: 15 minutes | Serves 2

2 medium potatoes

1 teaspoon butter

3 tablespoons sour cream

1 teaspoon chives

1½ tablespoons grated Parmesan cheese

1. Preheat the air fryer to 180ºC. 2. Pierce the potatoes with a fork and boil them in water until they are cooked. 3. Transfer to the air fryer and air fry for 15 minutes. 4. In the meantime, combine the sour cream, cheese and chives in a bowl. Cut the potatoes halfway to open them up and fill with the butter and sour cream mixture. 5. Serve immediately.

Flatbread

Prep time: 5 minutes | Cook time: 7 minutes | Serves 2

225 g shredded Mozzarella cheese

25 g blanched finely ground

almond flour

30 g full-fat cream cheese, softened

1. In a large microwave-safe bowl, melt Mozzarella in the microwave for 30 seconds. Stir in almond flour until smooth and then add cream cheese. Continue mixing until dough forms, gently kneading it with wet hands if necessary. 2. Divide the dough into two pieces and roll out to ¼-inch thickness between two pieces of parchment. Cut another piece of parchment to fit your air fryer basket. 3. Place a piece of flatbread onto your parchment and into the air fryer, working in two batches if needed. 4. Adjust the temperature to 160ºC and air fry for 7 minutes. 5. Halfway through the cooking time flip the flatbread. Serve warm.

Parmesan-Rosemary Radishes

Prep time: 5 minutes | Cook time: 15 to 20 minutes | Serves 4

1 bunch radishes, stemmed, trimmed, and quartered

1 tablespoon avocado oil

2 tablespoons finely grated fresh Parmesan cheese

1 tablespoon chopped fresh rosemary

Sea salt and freshly ground black pepper, to taste

1. Place the radishes in a medium bowl and toss them with the avocado oil, Parmesan cheese, rosemary, salt, and pepper. 2. Set the air fryer to190ºC. Arrange the radishes in a single layer in the air fryer basket. Roast for 15 to 20 minutes, until golden brown and tender. Let cool for 5 minutes before serving.

Courgette Fritters

Prep time: 10 minutes | Cook time: 10 minutes | Serves 4

2 courgette, grated (about 450 g)

1 teaspoon salt

25 g almond flour

20 g grated Parmesan cheese

1 large egg

¼ teaspoon dried thyme

¼ teaspoon ground turmeric

¼ teaspoon freshly ground black pepper

1 tablespoon olive oil

½ lemon, sliced into wedges

1. Preheat the air fryer to 200ºC. Cut a piece of parchment paper to fit slightly smaller than the bottom of the air fryer. 2. Place the courgette in a large colander and sprinkle with the salt. Let sit for 5 to 10 minutes. Squeeze as much liquid as you can from the courgette and place in a large mixing bowl. Add the almond flour, Parmesan, egg, thyme, turmeric, and black pepper. Stir gently until thoroughly combined. 3. Shape the mixture into 8 patties and arrange on the parchment paper. Brush lightly with the olive oil. Pausing halfway through the cooking time to turn the patties, air fry for 10 minutes until golden brown. Serve warm with the lemon wedges.

Baked Jalapeño and Cheese Cauliflower Mash

Prep time: 10 minutes | Cook time: 15 minutes | Serves 6

1 (340 g) steamer bag cauliflower florets, cooked according to package instructions	120 g shredded sharp Cheddar cheese
2 tablespoons salted butter, softened	20 g pickled jalapeños
	½ teaspoon salt
60 g cream cheese, softened	¼ teaspoon ground black pepper

1. Place cooked cauliflower into a food processor with remaining ingredients. Pulse twenty times until cauliflower is smooth and all ingredients are combined. 2. Spoon mash into an ungreased round nonstick baking dish. Place dish into air fryer basket. Adjust the temperature to 190ºC and bake for 15 minutes. The top will be golden brown when done. Serve warm.

Curried Fruit

Prep time: 10 minutes | Cook time: 20 minutes | Serves 6 to 8

210 g cubed fresh pineapple	425 g can dark, sweet, pitted cherries with juice
200 g cubed fresh pear (firm, not overly ripe)	2 tablespoons brown sugar
230 g frozen peaches, thawed	1 teaspoon curry powder

1. Combine all ingredients in large bowl. Stir gently to mix in the sugar and curry. 2. Pour into a baking pan and bake at 180ºC for 10 minutes. 3. Stir fruit and cook 10 more minutes. 4. Serve hot.

Shishito Pepper Roast

Prep time: 4 minutes | Cook time: 9 minutes | Serves 4

Cooking oil spray (sunflower, safflower, or refined coconut)	1 tablespoon soy sauce
450 g shishito, Anaheim, or bell peppers, rinsed	2 teaspoons freshly squeezed lime juice
	2 large garlic cloves, pressed

1. Insert the crisper plate into the basket and the basket into the unit. Preheat the unit by selecting AIR ROAST, setting the temperature to 200ºC, and setting the time to 3 minutes. Select START/STOP to begin. 2. Once the unit is preheated, spray the crisper plate and the basket with cooking oil. Place the peppers into the basket and spray them with oil. 3. Select AIR ROAST, set the temperature to 200ºC, and set the time to 9 minutes. Select START/STOP to begin. 4. After 3 minutes, remove the basket and shake the peppers. Spray the peppers with more oil. Reinsert the basket to resume cooking. Repeat this step again after 3 minutes. 5. While the peppers roast, in a medium bowl, whisk the soy sauce, lime juice, and garlic until combined. Set aside. 6. When the cooking is complete, several of the peppers should have lots of nice browned spots on them. If using Anaheim or bell peppers, cut a slit in the side of each pepper and remove the seeds, which can be bitter. 7. Place the roasted peppers in the bowl with the sauce. Toss to coat the peppers evenly and serve.

Parmesan-Thyme Butternut Squash

Prep time: 15 minutes | Cook time: 20 minutes | Serves 4

350 g butternut squash, cubed into 1-inch pieces (approximately 1 medium)	¼ teaspoon garlic powder
	¼ teaspoon black pepper
	1 tablespoon fresh thyme
2 tablespoons olive oil	20 g grated Parmesan
¼ teaspoon salt	

1. Preheat the air fryer to 180ºC. 2. In a large bowl, combine the cubed squash with the olive oil, salt, garlic powder, pepper, and thyme until the squash is well coated. 3. Pour this mixture into the air fryer basket, and roast for 10 minutes. Stir and roast another 8 to 10 minutes more. 4. Remove the squash from the air fryer and toss with freshly grated Parmesan before serving.

Maple-Roasted Tomatoes

Prep time: 15 minutes | Cook time: 20 minutes | Serves 2

280 g cherry tomatoes, halved	2 sprigs fresh thyme, stems removed
coarse sea salt, to taste	
2 tablespoons maple syrup	1 garlic clove, minced
1 tablespoon vegetable oil	Freshly ground black pepper

1. Place the tomatoes in a colander and sprinkle liberally with salt. Let stand for 10 minutes to drain. 2. Transfer the tomatoes cut-side up to a cake pan, then drizzle with the maple syrup, followed by the oil. Sprinkle with the thyme leaves and garlic and season with pepper. Place the pan in the air fryer and roast at 160ºC until the tomatoes are soft, collapsed, and lightly caramelized on top, about 20 minutes. 3. Serve straight from the pan or transfer the tomatoes to a plate and drizzle with the juices from the pan to serve.

Hasselback Potatoes with Chive Pesto

Prep time: 10 minutes | Cook time: 40 minutes | Serves 2

2 medium Maris Piper potatoes
5 tablespoons olive oil
coarse sea salt and freshly ground black pepper, to taste
10 g roughly chopped fresh chives
2 tablespoons packed fresh flat-

leaf parsley leaves
1 tablespoon chopped walnuts
1 tablespoon grated Parmesan cheese
1 teaspoon fresh lemon juice
1 small garlic clove, peeled
60 g sour cream

1. Place the potatoes on a cutting board and lay a chopstick or thin-handled wooden spoon to the side of each potato. Thinly slice the potatoes crosswise, letting the chopstick or spoon handle stop the blade of your knife, and stop ½ inch short of each end of the potato. Rub the potatoes with 1 tablespoon of the olive oil and season with salt and pepper. 2. Place the potatoes, cut-side up, in the air fryer and air fry at 190°C until golden brown and crisp on the outside and tender inside, about 40 minutes, drizzling the insides with 1 tablespoon more olive oil and seasoning with more salt and pepper halfway through. 3. Meanwhile, in a small blender or food processor, combine the remaining 3 tablespoons olive oil, the chives, parsley, walnuts, Parmesan, lemon juice, and garlic and purée until smooth. Season the chive pesto with salt and pepper. 4. Remove the potatoes from the air fryer and transfer to plates. Drizzle the potatoes with the pesto, letting it drip down into the grooves, then dollop each with sour cream and serve hot.

Mashed Sweet Potato Tots

Prep time: 10 minutes | Cook time: 12 to 13 minutes per batch | Makes 18 to 24 tots

210 g cooked mashed sweet potatoes
1 egg white, beaten
⅛ teaspoon ground cinnamon
1 dash nutmeg

2 tablespoons chopped pecans
1½ teaspoons honey
Salt, to taste
50 g panko bread crumbs
Oil for misting or cooking spray

1. Preheat the air fryer to 200°C. 2. In a large bowl, mix together the potatoes, egg white, cinnamon, nutmeg, pecans, honey, and salt to taste. 3. Place panko crumbs on a sheet of wax paper. 4. For each tot, use about 2 teaspoons of sweet potato mixture. To shape, drop the measure of potato mixture onto panko crumbs and push crumbs up and around potatoes to coat edges. Then turn tot over to coat other side with crumbs. 5. Mist tots with oil or cooking spray and place in air fryer basket in single layer. 6. Air fry at 200°C for 12 to 13 minutes, until browned and crispy. 7. Repeat steps 5 and 6 to cook remaining tots.

Fried Brussels Sprouts

Prep time: 10 minutes | Cook time: 18 minutes | Serves 4

1 teaspoon plus 1 tablespoon extra-virgin olive oil, divided
2 teaspoons minced garlic
2 tablespoons honey
1 tablespoon sugar
2 tablespoons freshly squeezed lemon juice
2 tablespoons rice vinegar

2 tablespoons sriracha
450 g Brussels sprouts, stems trimmed and any tough leaves removed, rinsed, halved lengthwise, and dried
½ teaspoon salt
Cooking oil spray

1. In a small saucepan over low heat, combine 1 teaspoon of olive oil, the garlic, honey, sugar, lemon juice, vinegar, and sriracha. Cook for 2 to 3 minutes, or until slightly thickened. Remove the pan from the heat, cover, and set aside. 2. Place the Brussels sprouts in a resealable bag or small bowl. Add the remaining olive oil and the salt, and toss to coat. 3. Insert the crisper plate into the basket and the basket into the unit. Preheat the unit by selecting AIR FRY, setting the temperature to 200°C, and setting the time to 3 minutes. Select START/STOP to begin. 4. Once the unit is preheated, spray the crisper plate with cooking oil. Add the Brussels sprouts to the basket. 5. Select AIR FRY, set the temperature to 200°C, and set the time to 15 minutes. Select START/STOP to begin. 6. After 7 or 8 minutes, remove the basket and shake it to toss the sprouts. Reinsert the basket to resume cooking. 7. When the cooking is complete, the leaves should be crispy and light brown and the sprout centres tender. 8. Place the sprouts in a medium serving bowl and drizzle the sauce over the top. Toss to coat, and serve immediately.

Fried Asparagus

Prep time: 5 minutes | Cook time: 12 minutes | Serves 4

1 tablespoon olive oil
450 g asparagus spears, ends trimmed
¼ teaspoon salt

¼ teaspoon ground black pepper
1 tablespoon salted butter, melted

1. In a large bowl, drizzle olive oil over asparagus spears and sprinkle with salt and pepper. 2. Place spears into ungreased air fryer basket. Adjust the temperature to 190°C and set the timer for 12 minutes, shaking the basket halfway through cooking. Asparagus will be lightly browned and tender when done. 3. Transfer to a large dish and drizzle with butter. Serve warm.

Turnip Fries

Prep time: 10 minutes | Cook time: 20 to 30 minutes | Serves 4

900 g turnip, peeled and cut into ¼ to ½-inch fries

2 tablespoons olive oil

Salt and freshly ground black pepper, to taste

1. Preheat the air fryer to 200ºC. 2. In a large bowl, combine the turnip and olive oil. Season to taste with salt and black pepper. Toss gently until thoroughly coated. 3. Working in batches if necessary, spread the turnip in a single layer in the air fryer basket. Pausing halfway through the cooking time to shake the basket, air fry for 20 to 30 minutes until the fries are lightly browned and crunchy.

Tofu Bites

Prep time: 15 minutes | Cook time: 30 minutes | Serves 4

1 packaged firm tofu, cubed and pressed to remove excess water

1 tablespoon soy sauce

1 tablespoon ketchup

1 tablespoon maple syrup

½ teaspoon vinegar

1 teaspoon liquid smoke

1 teaspoon hot sauce

2 tablespoons sesame seeds

1 teaspoon garlic powder

Salt and ground black pepper, to taste

Cooking spray

1. Preheat the air fryer to 190ºC. 2. Spritz a baking dish with cooking spray. 3. Combine all the ingredients to coat the tofu completely and allow the marinade to absorb for half an hour. 4. Transfer the tofu to the baking dish, then air fry for 15 minutes. Flip the tofu over and air fry for another 15 minutes on the other side. 5. Serve immediately.

Chapter 9 Vegetarian Mains

Chapter 9 Vegetarian Mains

Three-Cheese Courgette Boats

Prep time: 15 minutes | Cook time: 20 minutes |

Serves 2

2 medium courgette	cheese
1 tablespoon avocado oil	¼ teaspoon dried oregano
60 ml low-carb, no-sugar-added	¼ teaspoon garlic powder
pasta sauce	½ teaspoon dried parsley
60 g full-fat ricotta cheese	2 tablespoons grated vegetarian
60 g shredded Mozzarella	Parmesan cheese

1. Cut off 1 inch from the top and bottom of each courgette. 2.Slice courgette in half lengthwise and use a spoon to scoop out a bit of the inside, making room for filling. 3.Brush with oil and spoon 2 tablespoons pasta sauce into each shell. In a medium bowl, mix ricotta, Mozzarella, oregano, garlic powder, and parsley. 4.Spoon the mixture into each courgette shell. Place stuffed courgette shells into the air fryer basket. 5.Adjust the temperature to 180°C and air fry for 20 minutes. To remove from the basket, use tongs or a spatula and carefully lift out. 6.Top with Parmesan. 7.Serve immediately.

Cauliflower Steak with Gremolata

Prep time: 15 minutes | Cook time: 25 minutes |

Serves 4

2 tablespoons olive oil	60 g Parmesan cheese
1 tablespoon Italian seasoning	Gremolata:
1 large head cauliflower, outer	1 bunch Italian parsley
leaves removed and sliced	2 cloves garlic
lengthwise through the core	Zest of 1 small lemon, plus 1 to
into thick "steaks"	2 teaspoons lemon juice
Salt and freshly ground black	120 ml olive oil
pepper, to taste	Salt and pepper, to taste

1. Preheat the air fryer to 200°C. 2.In a small bowl, combine the olive oil and Italian seasoning. 3.Brush both sides of each cauliflower "steak" generously with the oil. 4.Season to taste with salt and black pepper. 5.Working in batches if necessary, arrange the cauliflower in a single layer in the air fryer basket. 6.Pausing halfway through the cooking time to turn the "steaks," air fry for

15 to 20 minutes until the cauliflower is tender and the edges begin to brown. 7.Sprinkle with the Parmesan and air fry for 5 minutes longer. 8.To make the gremolata: In a food processor fitted with a metal blade, combine the parsley, garlic, and lemon zest and juice. 9.With the motor running, add the olive oil in a steady stream until the mixture forms a bright green sauce. 10.Season to taste with salt and black pepper. 11.Serve the cauliflower steaks with the gremolata spooned over the top.

Garlicky Sesame Carrots

Prep time: 5 minutes | Cook time: 16 minutes |

Serves 4 to 6

450 g baby carrots	Freshly ground black pepper, to
1 tablespoon sesame oil	taste
½ teaspoon dried dill	6 cloves garlic, peeled
Pinch salt	3 tablespoons sesame seeds

1. Preheat the air fryer to 190°C. 2.In a medium bowl, drizzle the baby carrots with the sesame oil. 3.Sprinkle with the dill, salt, and pepper and toss to coat well. 4.Place the baby carrots in the air fryer basket and roast for 8 minutes. 5.Remove the basket and stir in the garlic. 6.Return the basket to the air fryer and roast for another 8 minutes, or until the carrots are lightly browned. 7.Serve sprinkled with the sesame seeds.

Crustless Spinach Cheese Pie

Prep time: 10 minutes | Cook time: 20 minutes |

Serves 4

6 large eggs	235 g shredded sharp Cheddar
60 ml double cream	cheese
235 g frozen chopped spinach,	60 g diced brown onion
drained	

1. In a medium bowl, whisk eggs and add cream. Add remaining ingredients to bowl. Pour into a round baking dish. Place into the air fryer basket. Adjust the temperature to 160°C and bake for 20 minutes. 2.Eggs will be firm and slightly browned when cooked. 3.Serve immediately.

Cheese Stuffed Peppers

Prep time: 20 minutes | Cook time: 15 minutes | Serves 2

1 red pepper, top and seeds removed	Salt and pepper, to taste
1 yellow pepper, top and seeds removed	235 g Cottage cheese
	4 tablespoons mayonnaise
	2 pickles, chopped

1. Arrange the peppers in the lightly greased air fryer basket. 2.Cook in the preheated air fryer at 200°C for 15 minutes, turning them over halfway through the cooking time. 3.Season with salt and pepper. 4.Then, in a mixing bowl, combine the soft white cheese with the mayonnaise and chopped pickles. 5.Stuff the pepper with the soft white cheese mixture and serve. 6.Enjoy!

Roasted Vegetable Mélange with Herbs

Prep time: 10 minutes | Cook time: 14 to 18 minutes | Serves 4

1 (230 g) package sliced mushrooms	3 cloves garlic, sliced
1 yellow butternut squash, sliced	1 tablespoon olive oil
1 red pepper, sliced	½ teaspoon dried basil
	½ teaspoon dried thyme
	½ teaspoon dried tarragon

1. Preheat the air fryer to 180°C. 2.Toss the mushrooms, squash, and pepper with the garlic and olive oil in a large bowl until well coated. 3.Mix in the basil, thyme, and tarragon and toss again. 4.Spread the vegetables evenly in the air fryer basket and roast for 14 to 18 minutes, or until the vegetables are fork-tender. 5.Cool for 5 minutes before serving.

Super Veg Rolls

Prep time: 20 minutes | Cook time: 10 minutes | Serves 6

2 potatoes, mashed	1 small onion, chopped
60 g peas	120 g breadcrumbs
60 g mashed carrots	1 packet spring roll sheets
1 small cabbage, sliced	120 g cornflour slurry (mix 40
60 g beans	g cornflour with 80 ml water)
2 tablespoons sweetcorn	

1. Preheat the air fryer to 200°C. 2.Boil all the vegetables in water over a low heat. 3.Rinse and allow to dry. 4.Unroll the spring roll sheets and spoon equal amounts of vegetable onto the centre of each one. 5.Fold into spring rolls and coat each one with the slurry and breadcrumbs. 6.Air fry the rolls in the preheated air fryer for 10 minutes. 7.Serve warm.

Super Vegetable Burger

Prep time: 15 minutes | Cook time: 12 minutes | Serves 8

230 g cauliflower, steamed and diced, rinsed and drained	tablespoons water, divided
2 teaspoons coconut oil, melted	1 teaspoon mustard powder
2 teaspoons minced garlic	2 teaspoons thyme
60 g desiccated coconut	2 teaspoons parsley
120 g oats	2 teaspoons chives
3 tablespoons flour	Salt and ground black pepper, to taste
1 tablespoon flaxseeds plus 3	235 g breadcrumbs

1. Preheat the air fryer to 200°C. 2.Combine the cauliflower with all the ingredients, except for the breadcrumbs, incorporating everything well. 3.Using the hands, shape 8 equal-sized amounts of the mixture into burger patties. 4.Coat the patties in breadcrumbs before putting them in the air fryer basket in a single layer. 5.Air fry for 12 minutes or until crispy. 6.Serve hot.

Pesto Vegetable Skewers

Prep time: 30 minutes | Cook time: 8 minutes | Makes 8 skewers

1 medium courgette, trimmed and cut into ½-inch slices	16 whole cremini or chestnut mushrooms
½ medium brown onion, peeled and cut into 1-inch squares	80 ml basil pesto
1 medium red pepper, seeded and cut into 1-inch squares	½ teaspoon salt
	¼ teaspoon ground black pepper

1. Divide courgette slices, onion, and pepper into eight even portions. 2.Place on 6-inch skewers for a total of eight kebabs. 3.Add 2 mushrooms to each skewer and brush kebabs generously with pesto. 4.Sprinkle each kebab with salt and black pepper on all sides, then place into ungreased air fryer basket. 5.Adjust the temperature to 190°C and air fry for 8 minutes, turning kebabs halfway through cooking. 6.Vegetables will be browned at the edges and tender-crisp when done. 7.Serve warm.

Courgette and Spinach Croquettes

Prep time: 9 minutes | Cook time: 7 minutes | Serves 6

4 eggs, slightly beaten

120 g almond flour

120 g goat cheese, crumbled

1 teaspoon fine sea salt

4 garlic cloves, minced

235 g baby spinach

120 g Parmesan cheese, grated

⅓ teaspoon red pepper flakes

450 g courgette, peeled and grated

⅓ teaspoon dried dill weed

1. Thoroughly combine all ingredients in a bowl. 2.Now, roll the mixture to form small croquettes. 3.Air fry at 170ºC for 7 minutes or until golden. 4.Tate, adjust for seasonings and serve warm.

Chapter 10 Desserts

Chapter 10 Desserts

Chickpea Brownies

Prep time: 10 minutes | Cook time: 20 minutes | Serves 6

Vegetable oil	cocoa powder
425 g can chickpeas, drained and rinsed	1 tablespoon espresso powder (optional)
4 large eggs	1 teaspoon baking powder
80 ml coconut oil, melted	1 teaspoon baking soda
80 ml honey	80 g chocolate chips
3 tablespoons unsweetened	

1. Preheat the air fryer to 160°C. 2. Generously grease a baking pan with vegetable oil. 3. In a blender or food processor, combine the chickpeas, eggs, coconut oil, honey, cocoa powder, espresso powder (if using), baking powder, and baking soda. Blend or process until smooth. Transfer to the prepared pan and stir in the chocolate chips by hand. 4. Set the pan in the air fryer basket and bake for 20 minutes, or until a toothpick inserted into the center comes out clean. 5. Let cool in the pan on a wire rack for 30 minutes before cutting into squares. 6. Serve immediately.

Cream-Filled Sandwich Cookies

Prep time: 8 minutes | Cook time: 8 minutes | Makes 8 cookies

Coconut, or avocado oil, for spraying	60 ml milk
1 tube croissant dough	8 Oreos
	1 tablespoon icing sugar

1. Line the air fryer basket with baking paper, and spray lightly with oil. 2. Unroll the dough and cut it into 8 triangles. Lay out the triangles on a work surface. 3. Pour the milk into a shallow bowl. Quickly dip each cookie in the milk, then place in the center of a dough triangle. 4. Wrap the dough around the cookie, cutting off any excess and pinching the edges to seal. You may be able to combine the excess dough to cover additional cookies, if desired. 5. Place the wrapped cookies in the prepared basket, seam-side down, and spray lightly with oil. 6. Bake at 180°C for 4 minutes, flip, spray with oil, and cook for another 3 to 4 minutes, or until puffed and golden brown. 7. Dust with the icing sugar and serve.

Gingerbread

Prep time: 5 minutes | Cook time: 20 minutes | Makes 1 loaf

Cooking spray	⅛ teaspoon salt
65 g All-purpose flour	1 egg
2 tablespoons granulated sugar	70 g treacle
¾ teaspoon ground ginger	120 ml buttermilk
¼ teaspoon cinnamon	2 tablespoons coconut, or
1 teaspoon baking powder	avocado oil
½ teaspoon baking soda	1 teaspoon pure vanilla extract

1. Preheat the air fryer to 160°C. 2. Spray a baking dish lightly with cooking spray. 3. In a medium bowl, mix together all the dry ingredients. 4. In a separate bowl, beat the egg. Add treacle, buttermilk, oil, and vanilla and stir until well mixed. 5. Pour liquid mixture into dry ingredients and stir until well blended. 6. Pour batter into baking dish and bake for 20 minutes, or until toothpick inserted in center of loaf comes out clean.

Double Chocolate Brownies

Prep time: 5 minutes | Cook time: 15 to 20 minutes | Serves 8

55 g almond flour	110 g unsalted butter, melted and cooled
25 g unsweetened cocoa powder	3 eggs
½ teaspoon baking powder	1 teaspoon vanilla extract
20 g powdered sweetener	2 tablespoons mini semisweet chocolate chips
¼ teaspoon salt	

1. Preheat the air fryer to 180°C. Line a cake pan with baking paper and brush with oil. 2. In a large bowl, combine the almond flour, cocoa powder, baking powder, sweetener, and salt. Add the butter, eggs, and vanilla. Stir until thoroughly combined (the batter will be thick.) Spread the batter into the prepared pan and scatter the chocolate chips on top. 3. Air fry for 15 to 20 minutes until the edges are set (the center should still appear slightly undercooked.) Let cool completely before slicing. To store, cover and refrigerate the brownies for up to 3 days.

Cream Cheese Shortbread Cookies

Prep time: 30 minutes | Cook time: 20 minutes | Makes 12 cookies

60 ml coconut oil, melted
55 g cream cheese, softened
100 g granulated sweetener
1 large egg, whisked

95g blanched finely ground almond flour
1 teaspoon almond extract

1. Combine all ingredients in a large bowl to form a firm ball. 2. Place dough on a sheet of plastic wrap and roll into a 12-inch-long log shape. Roll log in plastic wrap and place in refrigerator 30 minutes to chill. 3. Remove log from plastic and slice into twelve equal cookies. Cut two sheets of baking paper to fit air fryer basket. Place six cookies on each ungreased sheet. Place one sheet with cookies into air fryer basket. Adjust the temperature to 160°C and bake for 10 minutes, turning cookies halfway through cooking. They will be lightly golden when done. Repeat with remaining cookies. 4. Let cool 15 minutes before serving to avoid crumbling.

Pecan and Cherry Stuffed Apples

Prep time: 10 minutes | Cook time: 20 minutes | Serves 4

4 apples (about 565 g)
40 g chopped pecans
50 g dried tart cherries
1 tablespoon melted butter

3 tablespoons brown sugar
¼ teaspoon allspice
Pinch salt
Ice cream, for serving

1. Cut off top ½ inch from each apple; reserve tops. With a melon baller, core through stem ends without breaking through the bottom. (Do not trim bases.) 2. Preheat the air fryer to 180°C. Combine pecans, cherries, butter, brown sugar, allspice, and a pinch of salt. Stuff mixture into the hollow centers of the apples. Cover with apple tops. Put in the air fryer basket, using tongs. Air fry for 20 to 25 minutes, or just until tender. 3. Serve warm with ice cream.

Roasted Honey Pears

Prep time: 7 minutes | Cook time: 18 to 23 minutes | Serves 4

2 large Bosc pears, halved lengthwise and seeded
3 tablespoons honey
1 tablespoon unsalted butter

½ teaspoon ground cinnamon
30 g walnuts, chopped
55 g part-skim ricotta cheese, divided

1. Insert the crisper plate into the basket and the basket into the unit.

Preheat to 180°C. 2. In a 6-by-2-inch round pan, place the pears cut-side up. 3. In a small microwave-safe bowl, melt the honey, butter, and cinnamon. Brush this mixture over the cut sides of the pears. Pour 3 tablespoons of water around the pears in the pan. 4. Once the unit is preheated, place the pan into the basket. 5. After about 18 minutes, check the pears. They should be tender when pierced with a fork and slightly crisp on the edges. If not, resume cooking. 6. When the cooking is complete, baste the pears once with the liquid in the pan. Carefully remove the pears from the pan and place on a serving plate. Drizzle each with some liquid from the pan, sprinkle the walnuts on top, and serve with a spoonful of ricotta cheese.

Mini Peanut Butter Tarts

Prep time: 25 minutes | Cook time: 12 to 15 minutes | Serves 8

125 g pecans
55 g finely ground blanched almond flour
2 tablespoons unsalted butter, at room temperature
25 g powdered sweetener, plus 2 tablespoons, divided
120 g heavy (whipping) cream
2 tablespoons mascarpone

cheese
110 g cream cheese
140 g sugar-free peanut butter
1 teaspoon pure vanilla extract
⅛ teaspoon sea salt
85 g organic chocolate chips
1 tablespoon coconut oil
40 g chopped peanuts or pecans

1. Place the pecans in the bowl of a food processor; process until they are finely ground. 2. Transfer the ground pecans to a medium bowl and stir in the almond flour. Add the butter and 2 tablespoons of sweetener and stir until the mixture becomes wet and crumbly. 3. Divide the mixture among 8 silicone muffin cups, pressing the crust firmly with your fingers into the bottom and part way up the sides of each cup. 4. Arrange the muffin cups in the air fryer basket, working in batches if necessary. Set the air fryer to 150°C and bake for 12 to 15 minutes, until the crusts begin to brown. Remove the cups from the air fryer and set them aside to cool. 5. In the bowl of a stand mixer, combine the heavy cream and mascarpone cheese. Beat until peaks form. Transfer to a large bowl. 6. In the same stand mixer bowl, combine the cream cheese, peanut butter, remaining 50 g sweetener, vanilla, and salt. Beat at medium-high speed until smooth. 7. Reduce the speed to low and add the heavy cream mixture back a spoonful at a time, beating after each addition. 8. Spoon the peanut butter mixture over the crusts and freeze the tarts for 30 minutes. 9. Place the chocolate chips and coconut oil in the top of a double boiler over high heat. Stir until melted, then remove from the heat. 10. Drizzle the melted chocolate over the peanut butter tarts. Top with the chopped nuts and freeze the tarts for another 15 minutes, until set. 11. Store the peanut butter tarts in an airtight container in the refrigerator for up to 1 week or in the freezer for up to 1 month.

Chocolate Bread Pudding

Prep time: 10 minutes | Cook time: 10 to 12 minutes | Serves 4

Nonstick, flour-infused baking spray
1 egg
1 egg yolk
175 ml chocolate milk
2 tablespoons cocoa powder
3 tablespoons light brown sugar
3 tablespoons peanut butter
1 teaspoon vanilla extract
5 slices firm white bread, cubed

1. Spray a 6-by-2-inch round baking pan with the baking spray. Set aside. 2. In a medium bowl, whisk the egg, egg yolk, chocolate milk, cocoa powder, brown sugar, peanut butter, and vanilla until thoroughly combined. Stir in the bread cubes and let soak for 10 minutes. Spoon this mixture into the prepared pan. 3. Insert the crisper plate into the basket and the basket into the unit. Preheat the unit to 160°C. 4. cook the pudding for about 10 minutes and then check if done. It is done when it is firm to the touch. If not, resume cooking. 5. When the cooking is complete, let the pudding cool for 5 minutes. Serve warm.

Carrot Cake with Cream Cheese Icing

Prep time: 10 minutes | Cook time: 55 minutes | Serves 6 to 8

80 g All-purpose flour
1 teaspoon baking powder
½ teaspoon baking soda
1 teaspoon ground cinnamon
¼ teaspoon ground nutmeg
¼ teaspoon salt
3 to 4 medium carrots or 2 large, grated
120 g granulated sugar
35 g brown sugar
2 eggs
175 ml canola or vegetable oil
Icing:
225 g cream cheese, softened at room temperature
8 tablespoons butter, softened at room temperature
70 g icing sugar
1 teaspoon pure vanilla extract

1. Grease a cake pan. 2. Combine the flour, baking powder, baking soda, cinnamon, nutmeg, and salt in a bowl. Add the grated carrots and toss well. In a separate bowl, beat the sugars and eggs together until light and frothy. Drizzle in the oil, beating constantly. Fold the egg mixture into the dry ingredients until everything is just combined and you no longer see any traces of flour. Pour the batter into the cake pan and wrap the pan completely in greased aluminum foil. 3. Preheat the air fryer to 180°C. 4. Lower the cake pan into the air fryer basket using a sling made of aluminum foil (fold a piece of aluminum foil into a strip about 2-inches wide by 24-inches long). Fold the ends of the aluminum foil into the air fryer, letting them rest on top of the cake. Air fry for 40 minutes. Remove the aluminum foil cover and air fry for an additional 15 minutes or

until a skewer inserted into the center of the cake comes out clean and the top is nicely browned. 5. While the cake is cooking, beat the cream cheese, butter, icing sugar and vanilla extract together using a hand mixer, stand mixer or food processor (or a lot of elbow grease!). 6. Remove the cake pan from the air fryer and let the cake cool in the cake pan for 10 minutes or so. Then remove the cake from the pan and let it continue to cool completely. Frost the cake with the cream cheese icing and serve.

Shortcut Spiced Apple Butter

Prep time: 5 minutes | Cook time: 1 hour | Makes 1¼ cups

Cooking spray
500 g store-bought unsweetened applesauce
90 g packed light brown sugar
3 tablespoons fresh lemon juice
½ teaspoon kosher, or coarse sea salt
¼ teaspoon ground cinnamon
⅛ teaspoon ground allspice

1. Spray a cake pan with cooking spray. Whisk together all the ingredients in a bowl until smooth, then pour into the greased pan. Set the pan in the air fryer and bake at 170°C until the apple mixture is caramelized, reduced to a thick purée, and fragrant, about 1 hour. 2. Remove the pan from the air fryer, stir to combine the caramelized bits at the edge with the rest, then let cool completely to thicken. Scrape the apple butter into a jar and store in the refrigerator for up to 2 weeks.

Hazelnut Butter Cookies

Prep time: 30 minutes | Cook time: 20 minutes | Serves 10

4 tablespoons liquid monk fruit, or agave syrup
65 g hazelnuts, ground
110 g unsalted butter, room temperature
95 g almond flour
55 g coconut flour
55 g granulated sweetener
2 teaspoons ground cinnamon

1. Firstly, cream liquid monk fruit with butter until the mixture becomes fluffy. Sift in both types of flour. 2. Now, stir in the hazelnuts. Now, knead the mixture to form a dough; place in the refrigerator for about 35 minutes. 3. To finish, shape the prepared dough into the bite-sized balls; arrange them on a baking dish; flatten the balls using the back of a spoon. 4. Mix granulated sweetener with ground cinnamon. Press your cookies in the cinnamon mixture until they are completely covered. 5. Bake the cookies for 20 minutes at 150°C. 6. Leave them to cool for about 10 minutes before transferring them to a wire rack. Bon appétit !

Bourbon Bread Pudding

Prep time: 10 minutes | Cook time: 20 minutes | Serves 4

3 slices whole grain bread, cubed
1 large egg
240 ml whole milk
2 tablespoons bourbon, or peach juice

½ teaspoon vanilla extract
4 tablespoons maple syrup, divided
½ teaspoon ground cinnamon
2 teaspoons sparkling sugar

1. Preheat the air fryer to 130ºC. 2. Spray a baking pan with nonstick cooking spray, then place the bread cubes in the pan. 3. In a medium bowl, whisk together the egg, milk, bourbon, vanilla extract, 3 tablespoons of maple syrup, and cinnamon. Pour the egg mixture over the bread and press down with a spatula to coat all the bread, then sprinkle the sparkling sugar on top and bake for 20 minutes. 4. Remove the pudding from the air fryer and allow to cool in the pan on a wire rack for 10 minutes. Drizzle the remaining 1 tablespoon of maple syrup on top. Slice and serve warm.

Luscious Coconut Pie

Prep time: 5 minutes | Cook time: 45 minutes | Serves 6

100 g desiccated, unsweetened coconut, plus 25 g, divided
2 eggs
355 ml almond milk
100 g granulated sweetener
30 g coconut flour

55 g unsalted butter, melted
1½ teaspoons vanilla extract
¼ teaspoon salt
2 tablespoons powdered sweetener (optional)
120 g whipping cream, whipped until stiff (optional)

1. Spread 25 g of the coconut in the bottom of a pie plate and place in the air fryer basket. Set the air fryer to 180ºC and air fry the coconut while the air fryer preheats, about 5 minutes, until golden brown. Transfer the coconut to a small bowl and set aside for garnish. Brush the pie plate with oil and set aside. 2. In a large bowl, combine the remaining 100 g shredded coconut, eggs, milk, granulated sweetener, coconut flour, butter, vanilla, and salt. Whisk until smooth. Pour the batter into the prepared pie plate and air fry for 40 to 45 minutes, or until a toothpick inserted into the center of the pie comes out clean. (Check halfway through the baking time and rotate the pan, if necessary, for even baking.) 3. Remove the pie from the air fryer and place on a baking rack to cool completely. Garnish with the reserved toasted coconut and the powdered sweetener or whipped cream, if desired. Cover and refrigerate leftover pie for up to 3 days.

Dark Chocolate Lava Cake

Prep time: 5 minutes | Cook time: 10 minutes | Serves 4

Olive oil cooking spray
15 g whole wheat flour
1 tablespoon unsweetened dark chocolate cocoa powder
⅛ teaspoon salt

½ teaspoon baking powder
60 ml raw honey
1 egg
2 tablespoons olive oil

1. Preheat the air fryer to 190ºC. Lightly coat the insides of four ramekins with olive oil cooking spray. 2. In a medium bowl, combine the flour, cocoa powder, salt, baking powder, honey, egg, and olive oil. 3. Divide the batter evenly among the ramekins. 4. Place the filled ramekins inside the air fryer and bake for 10 minutes. 5. Remove the lava cakes from the air fryer and slide a knife around the outside edge of each cake. Turn each ramekin upside down on a saucer and serve.

Appendix Air Fryer Cooking Chart

Air Fryer Cooking Chart

Beef

Item	Temp (°F)	Time (mins)	Item	Temp (°F)	Time (mins)
Beef Eye Round Roast (4 lbs.)	400 °F	45 to 55	Meatballs (1-inch)	370 °F	7
Burger Patty (4 oz.)	370 °F	16 to 20	Meatballs (3-inch)	380 °F	10
Filet Mignon (8 oz.)	400 °F	18	Ribeye, bone-in (1-inch, 8 oz)	400 °F	10 to 15
Flank Steak (1.5 lbs.)	400 °F	12	Sirloin steaks (1-inch, 12 oz)	400 °F	9 to 14
Flank Steak (2 lbs.)	400 °F	20 to 28			

Chicken

Item	Temp (°F)	Time (mins)	Item	Temp (°F)	Time (mins)
Breasts, bone in (1 ¼ lb.)	370 °F	25	Legs, bone-in (1 ¾ lb.)	380 °F	30
Breasts, boneless (4 oz)	380 °F	12	Thighs, boneless (1 ½ lb.)	380 °F	18 to 20
Drumsticks (2 ½ lb.)	370 °F	20	Wings (2 lb.)	400 °F	12
Game Hen (halved 2 lb.)	390 °F	20	Whole Chicken	360 °F	75
Thighs, bone-in (2 lb.)	380 °F	22	Tenders	360 °F	8 to 10

Pork & Lamb

Item	Temp (°F)	Time (mins)	Item	Temp (°F)	Time (mins)
Bacon (regular)	400 °F	5 to 7	Pork Tenderloin	370 °F	15
Bacon (thick cut)	400 °F	6 to 10	Sausages	380 °F	15
Pork Loin (2 lb.)	360 °F	55	Lamb Loin Chops (1-inch thick)	400 °F	8 to 12
Pork Chops, bone in (1-inch, 6.5 oz)	400 °F	12	Rack of Lamb (1.5 – 2 lb.)	380 °F	22

Fish & Seafood

Item	Temp (°F)	Time (mins)	Item	Temp (°F)	Time (mins)
Calamari (8 oz)	400 °F	4	Tuna Steak	400 °F	7 to 10
Fish Fillet (1-inch, 8 oz)	400 °F	10	Scallops	400 °F	5 to 7
Salmon, fillet (6 oz)	380 °F	12	Shrimp	400 °F	5
Swordfish steak	400 °F	10			

Air Fryer Cooking Chart

Vegetables					
INGREDIENT	**AMOUNT**	**PREPARATION**	**OIL**	**TEMP**	**COOK TIME**
Asparagus	2 bunches	Cut in half, trim stems	2 Tbsp	420°F	12-15 mins
Beets	1½ lbs	Peel, cut in ½-inch cubes	1Tbsp	390°F	28-30 mins
Bell peppers (for roasting)	4 peppers	Cut in quarters, remove seeds	1Tbsp	400°F	15-20 mins
Broccoli	1 large head	Cut in 1-2-inch florets	1Tbsp	400°F	15-20 mins
Brussels sprouts	1lb	Cut in half, remove stems	1Tbsp	425°F	15-20 mins
Carrots	1lb	Peel, cut in ¼-inch rounds	1 Tbsp	425°F	10-15 mins
Cauliflower	1 head	Cut in 1-2-inch florets	2 Tbsp	400°F	20-22 mins
Corn on the cob	7 ears	Whole ears, remove husks	1 Tbps	400°F	14-17 mins
Green beans	1 bag (12 oz)	Trim	1 Tbps	420°F	18-20 mins
Kale (for chips)	4 oz	Tear into pieces, remove stems	None	325°F	5-8 mins
Mushrooms	16 oz	Rinse, slice thinly	1 Tbps	390°F	25-30 mins
Potatoes, russet	1½ lbs	Cut in 1-inch wedges	1 Tbps	390°F	25-30 mins
Potatoes, russet	1lb	Hand-cut fries, soak 30 mins in cold water, then pat dry	½ -3 Tbps	400°F	25-28 mins
Potatoes, sweet	1lb	Hand-cut fries, soak 30 mins in cold water, then pat dry	1 Tbps	400°F	25-28 mins
Zucchini	1lb	Cut in eighths lengthwise, then cut in half	1 Tbps	400°F	15-20 mins

Printed in Great Britain
by Amazon

25749843R00044